THE ENIGMA OF RABELAIS

THE ENIGMA OF RABELAIS

AN ESSAY IN INTERPRETATION

By A. F. CHAPPELL

CAMBRIDGE

AT THE UNIVERSITY PRESS

1924

CAMBRIDGE UNIVERSITY PRESS
Cambridge, New York, Melbourne, Madrid, Cape Town,
Singapore, São Paulo, Delhi, Mexico City

Cambridge University Press
The Edinburgh Building, Cambridge CB2 8RU, UK

Published in the United States of America by Cambridge University Press, New York

www.cambridge.org
Information on this title: www.cambridge.org/9781107636019

First published 1924
First paperback edition 2013

A catalogue record for this publication is available from the British Library

ISBN 978-1-107-63601-9 Paperback

'Rabelais surtout est incompréhensible; son livre est une énigme, quoiqu'on veuille dire, inexplicable; c'est une chimère, c'est le visage d'une belle femme avec des pieds et une queue de serpent ou de quelque autre bête plus difforme; c'est un monstrueux assemblage d'une morale fine et ingénieuse et d'une sale corruption. Où il est mauvais, il passe bien au delà du pire, c'est le charme de la canaille; où il est bon, il va jusques à l'exquis et à l'excellent, il peut être le mets des plus délicats.'

LA BRUYÈRE, *Les Caractères*, chap. I.

'Entre les livres simplement plaisants, je treuve des modernes, le Decameron de Boccace, Rabelais, et les Baisers de Jehan Second, *s'il les fault loger soubs ce tiltre*, dignes qu'on s'y amuse.'

MONTAIGNE, *Les Essais*, Livre II, chap. X.

NOTE

THE author wishes to thank most heartily Mr A. Tilley for the kindly interest he has long shown in the following work.

CONTENTS

ABBREVIATIONS USED

P.   *Pantagruel,* 1532; finally revised 1542. Edition quoted: reprint of *Pantagruel* (Edition de Lyon, Juste, 1533), edited by P. Babeau, J. Boulenger and H. Patry. Paris: Champion, 1904.

G.   *Gargantua,* 1534; finally revised 1542.

T.L.   *Tiers Livre,* 1546.

Q.L.   *Quart Livre,* 1552. In 1548 a portion of this book appeared.

A.P.   *Ancien Prologue* of *Quart Livre,* 1548.

I.S.   *Isle Sonante,* 1562, posthumous. Edition quoted: reprint. Edited by Lefranc and Boulenger. Paris: Champion, 1905.

R.E.R.   *Revue des Etudes Rabelaisiennes,* 1903–   .

R.S.S.   *Revue du Seizième Siècle.*

INTRODUCTORY

RABELAIS' purpose has been most variously interpreted. In appealing to men of very divergent
views in an age of theological debate his work
naturally aroused the bitterest enmity in many powerful minds; indeed it would seem to have brought
about a momentary alliance between the Catholics
and the Calvinists in consequence of his refusal to
be bound by their common principles. Therefore we
find both orthodox believers and the new sectaries
seeking to minimize this evil influence by denunciations of the teaching and even by vilification of the
teacher, and it is only of recent date that refutations
of the more extravagant legends thus generated have
appeared. Montaigne's hesitating opinion and La
Bruyère's still stranger criticism have not thrown
sufficient light upon the question, but they have
rather intensified the confusion. We must concede
that, so long as the work is considered as an organic
whole, Rabelais appears to be an enigma, but it is
essential that we should study the work as an expression of a mind developing under natural conditions
at a time when most men were powerfully affected
and disturbed. Rabelais must himself have developed,
and, since his work was so personal, that development must be traceable therein. It seems impossible
to reach the truth by tracing apparently Protestant

thought in the earlier portion, and then attempting to track such sympathy down in the later work; still less possible is it, on the authority of one or two passages, to explain the variety of the adventures by supposing that the skilled physician merely sought to amuse his patients, for the subject-matter is hardly conceivable as amusing, and when the above passages were written the author had been forced to adopt or had voluntarily adopted a figurative way of expression[1]. The real critical difficulty appears to arise out of the inadequate recognition of the years that followed the publication of *Gargantua* and preceded that of the *Tiers Livre*. It appears in the highest degree probable that, in those years of which little or nothing is known about his life (1534 or 1535 to 1546), the remarkable change in the author's circumstances altogether altered his views on life, a supposition not out of keeping with observed developments of the human mind even later in an individual's life.

Such a transformation may occur very gradually with the result that the individual himself is least aware of it. This appears to have been the fact in Rabelais, and the author of the *Tiers Livre* seems not at first to have noticed that his thought was not consonant with what his readers had been led to expect. Two years later, 1548, he published a fragment with a prologue, now printed as 'L'ancien

[1] See the use of 'vin' in extract from 'L'Ancien prologue,' *Q. L.*, quoted in the next paragraph.

prologue' of the *Quart Livre*, in which occurs the following curious passage:

Vous dictes. Quoy? *Que en rien ne vous ay fasché par tous mes livres cy devant imprimés.* Si à ce propos je vous allègue la sentence d'un ancien Pantagrueliste, encores moins vous fascheray. . . . Plus dictes que le vin du tiers livre a esté à vostre goust, et qu'il est bon. Vray est qu'il y en avoit peu, et ne vous plaist *ce que l'on dist communément,* un peu et du bon. Plus vous plaist. . . beaucoup et du bon.

And thereupon he passed on to write a passage in his untroubled joyous style, but the hesitancy and the wording of the italicized phrases are worthy of note. The author opens with the insinuation that he had not really offended his public, then he suggests that they will find the 'wine' to their taste and good, and finally he quotes the common criticism of his latest work. Only then does he concede his reader's demand for much of the good 'wine'; but in so doing he happens to use the word in a figurative sense, a distinct change from his practice of the early period. It cannot possibly be maintained that 'boire d'autant' meant originally anything but actual drinking, nor that the excellent 'Propos des Beuveurs' is at all incongruous in a story wherein one of the giants provokes thirst by his shadow falling upon a companion. In the earlier portion wine and drinking are to be taken literally; in the above passage wine is synonymous with delight. Under the circumstances a comparison of the tone and spirit of the 1548 volume with that of *Gargantua* and *Pantagruel* would appear natural and essential. This hurriedly published volume, later incorporated in the *Quart Livre*, consists of the opening chapter, Panurge's adventure with the sheep dealers (v–viii), the greater part of the storm episode (xviii–xx), Ennasin, Cheli, 'Pourquoi les moines sont voluntiers en cuisine' (in part), part of Procuration Island (ix–xii), Friar John's test of the Chiquanous (xvi), the death of Bringuenarilles[1], the sequel of the storm scene (xxi–xxiv), and part of the episode of the Macreons (xxv)[2]. This outline is perhaps sufficient to indicate a general resemblance in the 1548 volume to the earlier work of 1532–5, rather than to the *Tiers Livre*, action taking the place of discussion; and the manner of setting some of these diverting adventures into the completed *Quart Livre* reveals that peculiar combination of the serious with the amusing which from that date became typical of his writing. The humour of Book iv, says Millet, is that of a big child[3], and this criticism seems to be near the mark. The pleasant narrative of *Gargantua*, so different from the enquiries of the *Tiers Livre*, is never again a feature of the still later

[1] Introduced from *Le disciple de Pantagruel*, for the authenticity of which book see Tilley, *François Rabelais*, pp. 200–1.

[2] See Tilley, *François Rabelais*, pp. 99–100. References given above are to the *Q. L.*

[3] *François Rabelais* (Grands Ecrivains Français), p. 64.

work. Instead, there is an earnestness, as of conviction, alternating with the old comic horse-play; and this may have been forced upon him by the demands of his readers for more of their old 'wine.' Again, as we might expect, a wider gap separates the *Gargantua* from the *Tiers Livre* than separates that book from the later books, and these two facts may suggest that the volume of 1548 was published in order to re-establish the somewhat disappointed reader's confidence in an author whose purposes had radically changed[1]. That change took place before the resumption of the romance in 1546, and it brought with it both a loss of the earlier characteristics[2], and on the whole a considerable gain in more subtle humour.

It therefore appears most probable that we should study Rabelais' work with a threefold division in mind: *Pantagruel* and *Gargantua*, the work of his immaturity; the *Tiers Livre* and *Quart Livre*, that of his maturity; and the *Quint Livre*, which, composed at various times, appeared posthumously[3]. The

[1] It has been suggested that the volume was published in order to get a little money.

[2] Plattard, *L'Œuvre de Rabelais*.

[3] The *Isle Sonante*, it seems to me, must have been written while his memories of Rome were still fresh in his mind, and while he was under the protection of the du Bellays, who shared his views. It is much more of a *jeu d'esprit* than the Homenas episode, though more powerfully satirical; yet the debating and combative spirit is lacking. The rest of the book ranges from the very early, *if* authentic, *Isle des Esclots* to the arrival at the Oracle which probably dates about 1542-6. There are sufficient clearly marked traces of Rabelais' power and thought

most important epoch of development is that (1535–46) which separates the two sections revised by the author, but the last book must not be neglected. It will confirm our views with all the greater force in that Rabelais did not prepare for his readers' acceptance what was undoubtedly conceived with great earnestness.

to justify our accepting the whole of the *Quint Livre*, with the exception of short interpolations and inappropriate readings which prove lack of skill in the editor of the 1564 edition.

I. THE LIFE OF RABELAIS

His relations with Voulté[1]

IN the comparatively few facts that research has established it is impossible to trace adequately what happened to Rabelais during this long period of eleven years. Yet uncertainty upon this point renders the student's enquiries vain from the start, for—to make mention of what may prove to be a somewhat important consideration—Rabelais, whom in 1537 Dolet hailed as 'the glory of the healing art,' was afterwards supremely known as the philosophical author of *Pantagruel*[2]. The significance of this change may, it is true, be over-stressed, but when we compare the work done before and after this lapse of time, and when we note that in the interim the author's style had been transformed, that a definite purpose had been adopted, and that discussion rather than narration came to engross his attention, we are driven to the conclusion that some enquiry into those obscure years is necessary for our understanding of the mature worker and therefore of the earlier work itself. In the absence of other certain knowledge what was in fact a mere episode, Jean Voulté's brief and intimate friendship and his violent quarrel with Rabelais, may throw very valuable light upon the question.

[1] The substance of this chapter appeared under the heading 'Voulté's rupture with Rabelais' in *The Modern Language Review* of July, 1923.
[2] Petit de Julleville, *Histoire de la littérature française*, vol. IV.

What is ascertainable of Rabelais' life, as far as
directly concerns us, can be briefly summarized here.
He passed his early years in the monastery of Fon-
tenay-le-Comte[1] busy with Pierre Amy in the study
of Greek. Forced by his fellow-monks' persecution to
quit this seclusion in 1524, he may well have carried
with him considerable resentment against those who
had thwarted his congenial pursuit of learning, and
ten years later he appears still to have had aspirations
to a monastic life of cultured indolence uninterrupted
by the irksome duties imposed by the life and the
rules of a monastery[2]. In consequence of this hatred
of monks he would naturally fall into line with the
reformers[3], but, though we must infer much from
his writings, from his life between 1524 and 1530
no definite evidence in support of his sympathy is
yet forthcoming. In the latter year, he matriculated
at Montpellier and thenceforward for five years the
facts which we know[4] show that he was busy in the
study and practice of medicine and in preparing
medical works for publication at Lyons. His pro-

[1] In 1522 and 1534 he was described as a young man, in 1519
as 'frère mineur' of this monastery. See A. Tilley, *François
Rabelais*.

[2] See the Abbey of Thelema in *Gargantua*.

[3] Frequent seemingly sympathetic references occur in the
early books. In an *attack* on the Parisians he speaks of 'un bon
prescheur evangelique,' and 'Sorbone, où lors estoit, main-
tenant nest plus loracle de Leucece' (Lutetia), *G.* 17.

[4] In University records, Lyons printing, etc. In 1537-8 he
became Licentiate and Doctor, lectured and carried out two
anatomies on human bodies.

fessional enthusiasm and skill were building up a splendid reputation.

Notwithstanding this, in 1535 (and for the second time) he suddenly abandoned his post in a Lyons hospital without leave of absence, and after a short time the hospital authority appointed his successor. From letters[1] we know that he had accompanied Jean du Bellay to Rome, where he must have been familiar with conditions in the Papal Court which had provoked the luxurious and magnificent Paul III to attempt reforms. The new Cardinal, Jean du Bellay, helped his physician to obtain the letter of absolution (dated Jan. 17, 1536) of which he stood in need, and which allowed him to transfer to another monastery and to practise medicine out of charity employing neither knife nor cautery. He could then return to Lyons with greater security, in spite of the notorious Cardinal de Tournon's having succeeded the benevolent Pompone di Trivulce as governor of Lyons[2]. It was about this time apparently that he chose to enter the recently secularized Abbey

[1] See *Letters to the Bishop of Maillezais*, and Rabelais' preface to Marliani's *Topographia Romae*. In the *Letters* he notes down political news and gossip; gives interesting facts about the Pope's family; refers pityingly to the houses, churches and palaces that were destroyed to prepare a road for Charles V's entrance to Rome; and to the commission given him by the Bishop for seeds, etc. In asking for a further sum of money he describes his modest way of living.

[2] In August, 1537, the Cardinal apprehended Rabelais who had been writing 'to one of the greatest rascals in Rome,' and asked for the Chancellor's further instructions.

of Saint-Maur-des-Fossés, and so could be present at
the dinner given in honour of Dolet's pardon (March,
1537), at which, among the most famous scholars of
the time, was the poet Voulté. Of his life thenceforward to July, 1540, however, we know only that
he continued his medical work; that he was in the
royal suite at Aigues-Mortes (July 14–16, 1538),
whence he returned with his patron as far as Lyons;
and that on August 13, 1539, he was at Montpellier
acting as 'father' to a student. During his long interrupted life in the latter town he must have made the
acquaintance of Guillaume Pellicier, the princely and
liberal-minded Bishop, whose tastes—like those of
Jean du Bellay—lay in diplomacy, in the collection
of manuscripts, and in the study of natural history
rather than in his episcopal duties[1]; and we can hardly
doubt that Rabelais found in him a congenial spirit.
For their common interests drew from Pellicier three
letters[2] which show that Rabelais resided with
Guillaume du Bellay in Turin from July, 1540, and
that thence he made exploratory journeys into the
Swiss valleys[3]. Thus in the year which saw Langey's

[1] Rabelais' acquaintance with such Concordat ecclesiastics as
the Bishop of Montpellier and the Cardinal du Bellay must
have introduced him to Catholicism quite distinct from that
of ordinary Frenchmen. If so he could doubtless look upon
the beliefs of sincere transmontane Catholics as he describes
those of Homenas.
[2] Dated July 23 and Oct. 17, 1540, and May 20, 1541.
[3] There he sought plants for the Bishop. In Jan. 1541,
according to a letter of Jean de Boyssonné, he passed through
Chambéry; and he may have taken part in G. du Bellay's ex-
pedition of enquiry into Waldensian opinions (1540–1).

troubles and labours finally force him to relinquish the post in which he had done so much for France, Rabelais must have been in fairly constant and close attendance upon his great master, to whose death at St Symphorien there are two well-known references in the romance. We know moreover that Rabelais must have been in Lyons in 1542 in order to supervise the new edition of *Pantagruel* and *Gargantua* by Juste[1]; and to that period, too, belongs his important letter to Antoine Hullot which shows that he wished to renew his acquaintance with Plato. The next two or three years, however, tell us nothing of his movements; but he certainly held the post of Master of Requests at court for a time, and that would enable him in 1545 to obtain the king's permission to print the *Tiers Livre*, although the official condemnation was to be expected. And the royal imprimatur contains terms so benevolent and so flattering to Rabelais that his hurried flight to Metz, unprovided with funds—to judge from his appeal to the Cardinal du Bellay (February 1, 1546)—has always challenged explanations. Various suggestions have been put forward to account for it; but what is certain is that the family of his patrons had lost power for the time[2], that Rabelais had personal enemies who were only

---

[1] In the same year, also, a translation of Rabelais' *Stratagemata* appeared at Lyons. It was an eulogy of Guillaume du Bellay's work.
[2] In 1545 a secretary of the Cardinal du Bellay was convicted of heresy and burnt at Paris.

too eager to seize any occasion for revenge, and that he had always alluded slightingly in his known works to authorities whose persecutions were becoming bolder. It is not necessary therefore to suppose that he was a confirmed Protestant. Indeed the notorious Cardinal de Tournon had failed to convict his prisoner of heresy in 1537; and when we consider the whole romance we find—even in the posthumous work—that the traces of Protestant sympathy become slighter even than those in *Gargantua*. We might rather expect quite another development, and besides to adopt the opinion that Rabelais held Protestant beliefs would, it will be found, lead us into still deeper difficulties.

For if we briefly enquire into what contemporaries considered to be Rabelais' religious views, we shall find that at a much later date (1550) Jean Calvin claimed that both Desperiers and Rabelais had once belonged to the reforming party until their jests, which blasphemed 'the sacred pledge of eternal life,' had brought upon them spiritual blindness[1]. And there can be little doubt that the *Cymbalum Mundi* abounds in matter to justify a charge from which Rabelais' work appears almost free[2]. Indeed, were

[1] Cp. *De Scandalis*: 'Alii (ut Rabelaesus, Desperius et Goveanus) gustato Euangelio, eadem caecitate sunt percussi. Cur istud? nisi quia sacrum illud vitae eternae pignus, sacrilega ludendi aut ridendi audacia ante profanarant.' No doubt Calvin seized upon the two cases because they were well-known names, but the opinion is noteworthy.

[2] Except, perhaps, utterances in *Pantagruel*, dealt with later which seem to have escaped notice in that age.

not ample confirmation forthcoming that he was
also guilty of so dangerous an offence, Calvin's
denunciation might provoke our question. At the
same time in forming a judgment we must not forget
that Cop's notorious speech and the 'Affaire des
placards' had early torn the reforming movement
into two sections, that from 1534 onwards Calvinism
had dissociated itself from the moderate reformers
whom Calvin was to denounce as half-hearted, and
that among the Third Party[1] there had appeared a
distinct tendency to return to the bosom of Holy
Church. It becomes probable therefore that Rabelais,
as a 'reformer,' was rather left behind by advancing
Calvinism than that he became an apostate from that
creed. Moreover he does not seem to fall into the
class of men of letters whose Platonism led them to
look kindly on Catholic superstitions for, although
up to 1540 he seems to have been a Platonist, after
that date he certainly toyed with that philosophy in
a contemptuous manner, and had probably rejected
it. In point of fact, if we may judge by repeated
utterances in his later work, he became almost as
hostile to the doctrines of the Church as he was the

[1] Calvin adds an explanation of this phenomenon, in *Ex-
cusatio ad Nicodemitas* (1545): 'Tertius ordo ex iis constat qui
religionem quodammodo in philosophiam convertunt...sed
quieti ac securi expectant donec Ecclesia in tolerabilem statum
reformetur: ut autem in eam rem incumbunt, quia periculosum
est, adduci nequeunt; quidam etiam eorum ideas Platonicas
concipiunt de modo colendi Dei. Itaque bonam partem
Papisticarum superstitionum excusant....Hic ordo fere constat
ex literatis.'

avowed critic and enemy of Calvinism. We may be certain that he remarked the evidence of reaction which culminated in the Truce of Nice, and, if that be so, we must admire the tenacity of purpose with which he continued on his course. That alone would sufficiently explain the frequent dangers into which he plunged. There could be no middle course at that time; he who was not with the reactionary authorities was opposed to them, but whether the views to which he obstinately adhered were religious in their nature, nothing but close enquiry can reveal. And Voulté's life and the causes of his quarrel with Rabelais do provide a starting point from which we may begin the search.

A student and later a lecturer in the College of Guyenne, and from 1534 to 1536 in the Faculty of Toulouse, Jean Voulté[1] became a close associate of Dolet's friend, the liberal Jean de la Boyssonné, and of Gripaldi, the eminent jurist whose championing of free enquiry brought upon him both Calvinist and Catholic persecution. The law school of Toulouse being then a stronghold of the reactionaries, it is significant that under Boyssonné's influence the young lecturer renounced his legal career in favour of letters, and furthermore, having visited Lyons in 1536, that he there formed sincere friendships with Dolet and Rabelais. These facts must point to a certain measure

[1] See R. C. Christie, *Etienne Dolet, a Martyr of the Renaissance*, for further details.

of liberalism in the young poet,—it is possible through the study of Plato,—which, even if it were but the enthusiasm of a youth, appears strange when we consider that within two years, and at a time when reaction was triumphant, Voulté suddenly quarrelled with his friends, returned to the practice of the law in Paris, and was destined to find favour in the reactionary court circles. The few remaining years of his life, for he was assassinated by a personal enemy in 1542, are obscure, but does not that fact too seem to suggest that he had abjured his former errors and returned to the bosom of the Church?

Inspired with eager admiration, Voulté had hastened to defend the author of *Pantagruel* and *Gargantua*, whom he had heard stigmatized as a madman: 'Someone has affirmed,' he cried, 'that thy heart, O Rabelais, has been afflicted with madness, ·when indeed 'twas humour mingled with thy invention. I hold that he lied who said thy works ring with madness. Say, Rabelais, dost thou indeed sing so? He was a Zoilus armed with mad iambics, for thy writings breathe out not insanity but jests[1].' Such a view of the early books was probably shared by most

[1]   Qui rabie asseruit laesum, Rabelaese, tuum cor,
       adjunxit vero cum tua Musa sales:
       hunc puto mentitum, rabiem tua scripta sonare
       qui dixit; rabiem, dic Rabelaese, canis?
       Zoilus ille fuit rabidis armatus iambis;
       non spirant rabiem, sed tua scripta jocos.
Ad Rabelaesum (Joannis Vultei Epigrammatum lib. IV, Lyons, 1537). The charge of madness might well refer to the wildly extravagant writing in Pantagruel's judgment, *P.* pp. 42–3.

contemporaries, as also possibly by Montaigne, but
it would help to confirm our theory of Voulté's
inclination towards liberalism. There can be little
doubt that to the poet's mind Rabelais' ridicule of
the representatives of the past and his monstrous
laughter suggested no deeper meaning than the free
jests of Erasmus and Marot; and it must be remembered that it was the author himself who later constantly read profound wisdom into his early merriment,
and who therefore has somewhat confused our vision
of him. At that period contempt for the older age
bound together reformers and men of letters, and
probably it attracted the young poet to the side of
the founder of Pantagruelism. Very soon, however,
when sympathy and other circumstances had contributed to make them intimates, Voulté detected
and denounced what was and is Rabelais' real distinction, what in fact differentiates clearly between
him and his reforming associates. In a semi-jocular
poem the poet expresses emphatic disapproval of his
friend's insatiate thirst for knowledge, and that knowledge of a seriously dangerous kind[1]. We picture
Rabelais with an appeal for information ever on his

[1]   Scire cupis qui sim, qui vivam, quoque parente
       sim natus, quae sit patria, quique lares.
     Scire cupis nomenque meum, nomenque puellae,
       scire cupis vitae quod genus ipse sequar.
     . . . .
     Nil non scire cupis; sed dum cupis omnia scire,
       non satis et nimium scire, Rabella, cupis.
   Ad Rabellam (Joannis Vultei inscriptionum libri duo, Paris, 1538).

lips, maybe—in so far as instances are quoted—of
a sort trivial in the extreme, but probably, if we may
judge by the cautious hint of the last two verses,
often of a much more perilous kind. 'Thou desirest
to know too much and not enough' is a strange
reproof at a time when the acquisition of *learning*
was held in highest honour. It cannot have implied
medical or linguistic studies, and 'thou desirest to be
ignorant of nothing' seems to prove that it is rather
knowledge, that it implied a search for certainty in
matters in which Voulté approved of no enquiry, and
at which the friend dared no more than hint[1].

Having become so deeply concerned for his erring
friend's welfare, the poet never afterwards addressed
the various poems openly to him, and in these name-
less poems the hints became more outspoken and the
charges more definite. It must be recalled that
Pantagruel owed much to Lucian and that in consequence Rabelais was frequently denounced as 'the
disciple of Lucian.' Among religious people indeed
Lucianic came to be synonymous with Pantagruelist.
If then we recall the ponderously learned jokes of
the two early books, we shall be almost forced to the

The change in the name (Rabella for Rabelaesus) may *possibly*
be significant, but the obvious change to Rabula was made by
others.

[1] In the early books these forbidden meditations are rare, as
we might expect. Speaking of the invaders, however, *G.* 27,
he points out that while clergy and doctors tending the sick
of the plague died, the marauders took no harm, and adds:
'Dond vient cela messieurs? Pensez-y, je vous prie.'

conclusion that the poem 'In quendam irreligiosum
Luciani sectatorem[1]' probably contains carefully
veiled references to some episode in their intercourse.
From such a jest as that 'Christus was not in use
among the Latins' a Calvin or a Voulté probably
judged that Rabelais blasphemed against the sacred
pledge of everlasting life; and we cannot doubt that
the younger Rabelais was capable of such a joke
though nothing short of intimate knowledge of his
conversation could prove that it implied positive ir-
reverence. The poet, however, goes on to hint at
speculations which indicate either infidelity in the
utterer or at least non-acceptance of important
doctrines, and which in that age could be voiced only
in the closest intimacy. 'Dost thou doubt,' cries the
poet, 'that the crime of our fathers was atoned for
by a beloved victim[2]?' It may of course be a rhetorical

[1]   In libris quoteis meis loquor de
          Christo, hoc sit quasi nomen haud receptum.
          Rides, displiceo auribus tuisque,
          dicis nec Latio fuisse in ore
          nomen, nomine quo beatius non
          ullum est.   *Hendecasyllaborum libri quattuor*, 1538.
Perhaps the following passage from the Prologue, *T. L.*, may
refer to some such regretted episodes: 'Cestuy exemple me
fait entre espoir et crainte varier, doubtant que, pour contente-
ment propense, je rencontre ce que jabhorre...en lieu de les
servir, je les fasche; en lieu de les esbaudir, je les offense....
Advenant le cas, ne seroit ce pour chevreter (se mettre en colere)?
Autrefois est il advenu; advenir encores pourroit.'
[2]   Vah, adhuc dubitas scelus parentum
          tractum mortifero asperoque morsu
          esse victima amabili expiatum?

development of the original offensive jest or it may be that Rabelais' desire for knowledge had led him into deep meditations, but we must admit that early or late his confidence in the goodness of human nature would drive him to question this orthodox tenet. For a much smaller matter Etienne Dolet laid down his life, and with rumours of such meditations possibly reaching the ears of the authorities in spite of the utmost discretion in his published work, we cannot wonder that Rabelais had often to seek safety in flight; we cannot be surprised if spies reported to the ecclesiastical powers otherwise than in accordance with *Pantagruel* and *Gargantua*[1]. Yet it is remarkable that the gross ribaldry of the earlier book did not apparently reveal to contemporaries the author's lack of religious convictions as it does to modern readers. The explanation is probably that against the background of the lower moral earnestness of the day such an element had not been prominent, and the author's scepticism was betrayed, unlike Dolet's, only in less guarded relationships. Voulté's horror at this discovery impelled him to make fruitless attempts to dissuade the poor 'Lucianicque' from pursuing a course dangerous to body and soul. In vain, he cries, will his friend postpone repentance. The evil day

[1] The Prologue, *T. L.*, contains references to the various persecutors seeking for slips in his writing: 'Arriere, mastins! hors de la quarriere! hors de mon soleil, cahuaille du diable.... Pourtant, arriere, cagotz! Aux ouailles, mastins! Hors dicy, caphards, de par le diable, hay!' etc.

when pretence and legalism will fail him[1] must arrive
bringing the bitterest regrets, and on the Last Day
he will recall his quondam friend's efforts at persuasion[2]. Only by fully comprehending the peculiar
trend of thought of those days could we hope to
realize the import of such passionate pleading. When
however we consider that men held tenaciously to
the revealed word and that doctrinal questions were
productive of the most violent disruptions of society,
and even of families, nay, of treacherous massacres
of men, women and children of a different faith,—

> slaughter'd saints, whose bones
> Lie scattered on the Alpine mountains cold,—

we can hardly hesitate to believe that, in rejecting
his friend's pleadings, Rabelais was either harder of
heart than his readers will trace in his works, or
more boldly resolved on his speculations than many
present views will easily allow. The truth probably
lies between these not exclusive explanations. Rabelais

[1]   Belle te simulasse Christianum.
       Rides, has rogo, pone, pone technas
       et subterfugia omnia; invidere
       hanc noli tibi quam impetrare possis
       criminis veniam, fatere mentem
       insani hactenus esse Luciani,
       vitam denique te impie secutum.
    In Luciani Simium (Hendecasyllaborum libri quattuor).

[2]   Dices: hei mihi, jam miser miser sum.
       Erravi, fateor, Deum esse nosco.
       Vixi, non homo, sed canis; poeta
       Vulteius mihi providus, poeta
       verax, hanc mihi centies ruinam
       hanc praedixerat.   (*Ibid.*)

was neither hard-hearted nor truly a profound thinker at that time, but he was developing in a noteworthy manner.

Enough may have been quoted to show that Voulté must not be considered as a moderate reformer who lightly turned back before threatened persecution, and who therefore quarrelled with his friend. The quarrel took place only when his dissuasive powers had failed, and when he feared to be involved in the eternal consequences of the daring enquiries to which Rabelais was much inclined. His poems are the cries of alarm uttered by a singularly devout man, who recoiled, and tried to drag back his friend, from the abyss of infidelity that lay before them. As for Rabelais, his position may be adequately explained only with reference to his new philosophy of Panta-gruelism, the boldness and courage of which lie hidden beneath his famous definitions[1] and descriptions of it, which must have exerted a powerful influence upon him at that time.

From the facts of his career we may now some-what amplify our conception of Rabelais' personality. His nature was largely moulded by life in a pro-vincial monastery into which the most liberal thought available to him necessarily penetrated by way of classical literature, and we can therefore dimly ap-

[1] During his *saddest* years, he defined it as 'a certain gaiety of mind composed of contempt of chance circumstances,' *Q. L.* Prologue.

preciate his obstinate prosecution of studies which
gave him a sense of living. Apart from that, however,
he probably spent this portion of his life to no greater
purpose than did most of his fellows[1]. Having entered
the world he had carried on various scientific studies,
he had been attached to two of the least prejudiced
nobles of his time, and he had travelled extensively
when opinions were in a ferment. We may be sure
from a study of *L'Isle Sonante* that, when he had
seen the actual state of the Church in Rome[2] at that
time, a considered and steadfast judgment took the
place of his fluctuating and traditional views, and this
fact prompts the question, How widely must his
opinions in other matters have changed? He had been
forced from the cavern, in which he had beheld the
merest shadows of a shadowy world, to look upon
reality in the broad light of day; and so far-reaching
a change from secluded idleness to private and public
activity cannot but have influenced him, perhaps even
transformed him by at first, no doubt, throwing his
thoughts into confusion. The change must certainly
have been painful. And it must be recalled that the
most potent influences which might have resolved

[1] Millet (*François Rabelais—*Les Grands Écrivains Français)
says that he was not in advance of his age on the question of
woman. See later chapter.

[2] Paul III, who later excommunicated Henry VIII, had set
himself to reform the Curia in 1534. When Rabelais visited
Rome with Jean du Bellay these reforms must have produced
much discontent and, moreover, that very idle purposelessness
of which the *I. S.* gives so fine a picture.

his doubts were brought to bear upon him after the publication of his two early books and still more after his acquaintance with Voulté. *Pantagruel* and *Gargantua* are therefore the utterances of the monk and the student; his later works those of the experienced man of the world.

During the first period his thought had of necessity followed the beaten tracks of Renaissance learning, and in consequence of his reverence for Erasmus, for whom he felt as a son for his father—nay, for his mother[1], he had dreamed of the world being reformed through the absorption of learning. He was of the opinion that students need but expound ancient philosophy, nay merely amass ancient knowledge, in order to equip princes for the right government of kingdoms. Such influences and such enthusiasms, which he held in common with many of his contemporaries[2], made a deep impression on his first two books. In the world, however, nothing but disillusionment fell to his lot: he saw the great and powerful dictating their pleasure to the weak; he must have realized that reform of human institutions became more and more difficult; and he probably would discover that the strength or weakness of human kind lay in an irrational objection to his reasonable reforms. Within a very few years the

[1] *Epistola ad B. Salignacum.*
[2] Dolet's Prefaces (quoted in Christie, *Etienne Dolet*) make mention of this feature of his age as though it were universally accepted.

2

author of *Gargantua* saw one ideal after another crushed beneath triumphant reaction[1], and it is not surprising that his disconcerted mind should strive to understand what might be the most powerful motives that urged onwards himself and his fellows. With his dream world shattered about him, Rabelais was compelled to seek a firm footing even in the most perilous places, and to such a man, prone to discouragement as Rabelais certainly was[2], a life of activity and of acquaintance with experienced men would be of the utmost importance in re-establishing mental calm. It was just when he most needed calm, and before he was to undergo Guillaume du Bellay's powerful influence, that Voulté knew him.

As a corrective to despair he had something more than his great patron's personal example. Whenever in his early work he recalls home scenes and homely or personal adventures, his style becomes rich and powerfully affective, while when treating of abstractions he seems to have felt hesitant and doubtful[3]. The artificial mode of life into which he had been forced, possibly when very young[4], had not weakened,

---

[1] After the interview at Aigues-Mortes.

[2] The Prologues fully testify to Rabelais' disappointments, cf. Prol. *Q. L.*

[3] When the realistic Panurge comes upon the scene, Pantagruel is for a long time lost sight of: nearly half of his first book is concerned primarily with Panurge. And though Friar John did not in the same way engross the author's attention, yet his appearance also *enlivens* the narration.

[4] Editus' utterance (*I. S.* p. 11) is generally accepted as

and had probably strengthened, this longing for fact and experience. Now, among all the elements of the story realism alone remains constant, and in such a period of mental upheaval no other quality could conceivably have been more valuable to him. No other power than that of interesting himself in the physical world could so well have carried him through to the time when he 'saw life steadily and saw it whole.' On what still remained certain he could take his stand and thence he could push his researches into the unknown. We must, with considerable advantage, accept the *Tiers Livre* as a résumé of part of Rabelais' enquiries, and in a similar way we must see in Pantagruel's later quest of truth[1] further revelations of what the author's life had taught him. Some of his enquiries have been referred to in his friend Voulté's poems.

The Pantagruel of his later books says:

Not without reason, it seems to me, did Nature fashion our ears open, putting over them no door nor any other

autobiographical. Note also how fondly he recalls childish experiences.

[1] Rabelais' interest in geographical discovery accounts for the form that he adopted but not for the matter. In *Pantagruel* the prince made a journey by sea from Paris to Utopia (*P.* p. 79); the place-names are either geographical (Madeira, Canary Islands) or various descriptions of nowhere and nothing (Meden, Uti, Gelasim, Achorie). The 1542 revision of *P.* possibly suggested the same notion with however places like *Procuration, Papefiguière, Papimanie* and *the manor of Messer Gaster*, i.e. Rabelais' thoughts on Protestants, Catholics, etc.

kind of barrier as she did in the case of the eyes, the tongue and other issues from the body. I think the reason is so that always and at all time we may continually hear and through hearing may be always learning[1].

Surely this rejoinder to Epistemon, who feared to consult witches, is no other than that with which Rabelais could have met Voulté's protests. 'What harm is there in knowing and constantly learning, even if it were from a fool, a pot, a flagon, mittens or a slipper?' What harm, indeed, can come of knowing and seeking to understand? A Calvin may prefer that all knowledge should vanish from the earth rather than that it should become a cause of stumbling to the faithful[2]; a Voulté may consider that all enquiry may be and should be confined within conventional bounds; but Rabelais could adopt neither course. His desire for knowledge, which seems to have horrified his friend and to have disrupted their friendship, he could not dominate; perhaps he himself could not at that time appreciate what was to give consistency to his later work, and what was to make the prudential

---

[1] *T. L.* 16. 'Nature me semble, non sans cause, nous avoir forme oreilles ouvertes, ny apposant porte ne clousture aucune, comme a faict es yeulx, langue et aultres issues du corps. La cause je cuide estre, afin que tousjours, toutes nuytz, continuellement puissions ouïr, et, par ouye, perpetuellement apprendre...
...Que nuist sçavoir tousjours et tousjours apprendre, fust ce
    D'un sot, d'un pot, d'une guedoufle,
    D'une moufle, d'une pantoufle?'

[2] Cp. *De Scandalis:* 'ego enim mallem, et certe praestaret, scientias omnes exterminatas è mundo esse, quam ut studio gloriae Dei Christianos alienent.'

revision of 1542 far from a satisfactory task[1]. Whereas the two early books, compared with the later romance, appear to be a conventional narrative, in the interest of his enforced speculation Rabelais had apparently prepared to push aside the most cherished beliefs of the day. We cannot wonder that Voulté should fail to realize how fundamental such a development would be. Indeed if a definite breach with the past had been made, only a careful comparison of the thought in the books produced before and after this critical period could reveal a most extraordinary interruption of Rabelais' development.

[1] Rabelais' additions in the 1542 revised edition throw a light upon this question. To the account of the giant Hurtaly sitting astride on the Ark and talking to its occupants (*P*. p. 9) he added: 'Avez vous bien le tout entendu? Beuvez donc un bon coup sans eau. Car si ne le croyez, non fais je fit elle' (*P*. c. 1). Much of the natural confusion on the question of Rabelais may possibly be explained by such wilful extravagance, though other explanations appear probable.

2. RABELAIS' HUMOUR

BEFORE proceeding however to consider the developments of Rabelais' main interests we shall find an advantage in attempting to dissociate, as far as may be, his subject-matter from his way of thinking and the expression of his thought. Only thereby may we hope to avoid the many pitfalls that lie about the path of those who seek to track down his social, religious and philosophic views. Indeed in the study of this philosophic romance so important is a sound understanding of the author's humour that many well-intentioned readers have failed to pierce through the ephemeral and reach the more lasting elements of the thought. To consider that the work as a whole was a mere amusement to the author, or even the convenient means of pandering to the taste of the vulgar, is to lose in jovial merriment the main truths that the author's life has revealed to us.

Certainly *Pantagruel,* the sequel to the *Grandes Cronicques* of which 'more copies were sold in two months than Bibles in nine years,' must appear to us to have been composed with no other intention than diversion. In spite of his assertion that he sought to make the second book more probable than the other[1], we can with difficulty recognize in the author either

---

[1] Speaking of the *Grandes Cronicques,* he says: 'Voulant doncques moy vostre humble esclave accroistre voz passetemps davantaige, Je vous offre de present ung aultre livre de mesme billon, sinon quil est ung peu plus equitable et digne de foy que nestoit lautre' (*P.* p. 4).

the man who was to write *Gargantua* or the transformed personality of the later work. There are indeed connecting threads between *Pantagruel* and
Gargantua, nay in the early books there are germs
of the later most puzzling developments, but the
slightest perusal would reveal wide differences. It is
not accidental that he should have so glorified eating
and drinking, for on a wider view of his work it will
be seen to be at least probable that his conversation
at table furnished the materials for his books. Indeed
he outlines this method of composition in the Prologue
of the *Tiers Livre*[1]; and there are signs in abundance
to confirm this opinion quite apart from the jest
which offended Voulté. At such times the runaway
monk's character was revealed without shame, his
secret speculations no doubt came to his lips, and his
extraordinary extravagance found favour with his
fellows. This was the Rabelais of the early books,
copious of invention, without restraint and from time
to time unexpectedly rash, but always tending from
abstractions to the grosser realities of the time.

The nature of the adventures in *Pantagruel* may
have been imposed upon him by the success of his
earlier venture, as we have seen above, and he planned
to continue them in a sequel[2]; and although in the

[1] 'Icy beuvant, je delibere, je discours, je resouldz et con-
cluds, Après lepilogue je ris, jescris, je compose, je boy,' and he
quotes justificatory examples from the Ancients.
[2] 'Comment Panurge fut marié, et coqu des le premier moys
de ces nopces; et Comment pantagruel trouva la pierre philoso-

summary of adventures that he promises we may no
doubt trace signs of the author's higher interests
which might lead on to his higher achievements, it
is obvious that Pantagruel was destined to occupy a
place among the commonplace heroes of the older
popular stories[1]. Hardly by anyone but a master of
his craft could the elements of the preceding story
be so tersely outlined, and it is clear that what he
stood most in need of in order to pen his later works
was a wider, and perhaps a nobler, but certainly a
more serious point of view. From the summary, however, as from the whole book, a very significant fact
emerges: it is that in 1533 the realistic Panurge, and
not his giant master, dominated the author's mind.
His self-chosen task of continuing the *Grandes
Cronicques* had proved too much for Rabelais. He
repeatedly abandoned the gigantic and had to return
to it with an effort. Thus, after the narration of the
prince's monstrous infancy and still more monstrous
life[2], after his brutal treatment of all inferiors from

phalle et la maniere pour la trouver et la maniere d'en user; et
comment il passa les montz Caspies, comment il navigua par la
mer Athlanticque, et deffist les Canniballes, et conquesta les
isles de Perlas...comment il combatoit contre les diables, et feist
brusler cinq chambres d'enfer, et mist a sac la grant chambre
noire, et getta Proserpine au feu, et rompit quatre dentz a
Lucifer,' etc. (*P.* pp. 109–10).

[1] See analysis of popular giant hero in J. Plattard, *L'Œuvre
de Rabelais*.

[2] Like Grippeminauld, though that monster did not *pro-
claim* the fact, Pantagruel devours little children ('car cest moy
qui mange les petitz enfans,' *P.* p. 83). Note how in the interval

the Limousin student, whom he seized by the throat
for latinizing French, to Humevesne and the audience
in his debate with Thaumaste, he was represented
as touched with pity at sight of the vagrant Panurge
('car jay affection tres grande de vous donner ayde
a mon pouvoir en la calamite ou je vous voy: car
vous me faictes grant pitie'). Again, explicitly compared with Hercules who cleansed the world of
monsters, he was a giant of respectable size whose
tongue might shelter an army from a rain storm, and
yet he was more profoundly affected than the very
human Panurge by the religious questions of the day;
he erected a trophy to God who heard his prayers
during the battle; and further he preached trust in
God to his prisoners[1]. In so far as the story was in
any part 'more worthy of belief' than the *Grandes
Cronicques*, it must have been in that section which
describes student life and the places that had come
into Rabelais' experience, but the result of this inter-
mingling of fact and fiction was a more confused
mass of amusing stories. It was not out of keeping
with his avowed intention, historically considered,
that a student of ancient literature should ridicule

between the *Pantagruel* and the *Isle Sonante*, this habit is transferred from the 'heroic' to the horrible. Panurge's appearance
relieves this oppressive element in this book.

[1] 'Mais je te dys, metz tout ton espoir en Dieu, et il ne te
delaissera poinct. Car de moy encores que soye puissant comme
tu peuz veoir, et aye gens infinitz en armes, toutesfois je ne espe
poinct en ma force, ny en mon industrie: mais toute ma fiance
est en dieu mon protecteur' (*P.* p. 89).

medieval institutions, and from this and the suc-
ceeding book a crude polemic may be disentangled[1].
In laughing at all that represented the past he displayed an ingenuity that is bewildering to modern
minds, but the objects that he judged worthy of his
ridicule are even more remarkable than his merriment. In his humorous references to the Church,
the Sorbonne, Scholasticism (the library of St Victor)
and the mysteries of Thaumaste's sign language we
shall search in vain for indications of the real Rabelais.
In fact his narrations were as medieval in tone and
style as the institutions that he attacked. By serious
students of that period his book might, no doubt, be
read as a distraction from their labours, by ordinary
readers with the same interest as they found in the
common story of magic, but it is almost incredible
that apart from the Sorbonne and the legal profession
it could arouse real hostility, or that it could appeal
to earnest minds. Be his professional and other interests
what they might be, his point of view seems to have
been in little nobler than that of his everyday acquaintance. For all practical purposes his book was
of the past, and so when he plunges into the account
of Epistemon's visit to Hell, or into the microcosmic
narrative of the author's journey in the giant's mouth,
which was repeated by 'the pilgrims in the salad' of
Gargantua, he cannot avoid the fault of over-elabora-
tion. Now his use of story and anecdote never

[1] Christie, *Etienne Dolet*, pp. 192–3.

diminished, but rather increased in his later books. The difference between his early and late practice is that, whereas later the stories were strictly subordinate and pertinent to a discussion or an event, earlier they are the stuff of his writing. Certainly Rabelais' skill in writing must have increased but that will not alone account for the superiority of the other books to *Pantagruel*. When we compare the episode of the 'haulte dame de Paris' with the anecdotes of the inquisitive nuns or the Lord of Basché, and only then, may we appreciate in the latter the appropriate subordination to thought and purpose, which alone gives point to modern story-telling, and which was quite absent from the former.

In composing the vastly superior *Gargantua*, in which he was still engaged upon the task of discrediting the past[1],—a purpose which may have caused the indulgence in much of the old rabelaiserie,—he seems to have realized this fault in *Pantagruel*. In the new book he had a worthier purpose in the exposition of Platonism[2], and so his narrative gained in strength and interest. But the great change in tone was largely owing to a visit to his native country ('mon pays de vache') which enlivened his language to a glow of personal concernment, which transformed his giants into bourgeois and tyrannical govern-

---

[1] The scheme of Education is an onslaught on that of Holofernes, and the Abbey of Thelema on monasticism.
[2] Cp. the verses addressed to the reader.

ment into commonplace benevolence, and which in
general enabled the author to descend from ideal
vaguenesses to reality[1]. It is probable that Rabelais'
genius prevented his excelling in ideal description
though not in the caricature of the ideal by the
addition of the real, and his life in Lyons had
somewhat checked his coarseness and had given
him greater scope for his peculiar bent. Consequently the genial bourgeois in him could portray
the scene of the drinkers (G. 5) and the monk's
diverting conversation at table (G. 39). He could
give utterance to such quips as 'which was first,
thirst or drinking?' ('Qui fut premier soif ou
beuverie? Soif car qui eust beu sans soif durant le
temps d'innocence'—G. 5), and to confessions that
'grapes with fresh cakes make divine meat' ('cest
viande celeste manger a desjeuner raisins avec fouace
fraische'—G. 25)[2]. Pantagruelism still implied and
taught drinking as much as you please ('boire
d'autant')[3], and when the Tourangeau urged his

[1] For a full account of the effects of this visit see Lefranc,
Introduction to *Gargantua*, pp. liv–lxxxvii, and a series of
articles in *R. E. R.*

[2] In *G.* 9, 10 we probably have one of Rabelais' after-dinner
topics treated in his best manner and revealing his fertile wit.

[3] In the 1534 edition of *Pantagruel* appears for the first time
a passage stating that the clergy spend their time making good
cheer and reading the Pantagruelist books (*P.* c. 34). It appears
that he had his doubts on the score of that book even then, and
later (*A. P.*) he makes the same charge with, however, considerable difference. In *G.*, Janotus de Bragmardo, wishing for
Gargantua's favour, sighs for 'bon vin, bon lict, le dos au feu,
le ventre a table' (*G.* 19).

readers to break the dry bones so as to get at the
marrow we may judge that he spoke with his tongue
in his cheek ('Puis, par curieuse leçon et meditation
frequente, rompre l'os et sugcer la substantifique
mouelle'). There is no 'dryness' while there are
instances in the book where the mask of profound
meaning is thrown off[1]. The stories are told with perfect equanimity and with complete enjoyment, and
so much is this the case that the author cares little
for critics who charge him with drunkenness[2]. True
there is a 'hidden doctrine' in *Gargantua*, and in
those sections where Rabelais teaches Platonism his
native grossness becomes both less in quantity and
less offensive than in *Pantagruel*, but in both books
the author is entirely satisfied with story-telling and
he lacks the critical spirit which might have considerably hampered his narrative genius.

With the *Tiers Livre* there came a change from
idle or didactic narration to debatings and discussions.
The action almost dried up or merely trickled where
before a torrent had carried the readers headlong.
With the *Quart Livre* action and amusement were
subtly combined with enquiry into profounder problems, and consequently there was necessarily a

[1] Friar John rejects Gargantua's recondite interpretation of
the enigma.
[2] Speaking of Horace he says: 'un malautru a dict que ses
carmes sentoient plus le vin que lhuile. Autant en dit un
Turlupin de mes livres; mais bren pour luy. L'odeur du vin,
ô combien plus est friant, riant, priant, plus celeste et delicieux
que d'huile' (Prol. *G.*).

change in manner. Not only was the mad incon-
sequential joy of living no longer possible, nor the
jovial exposition of ideas dear to the author, but
from that date onwards he seems to have lost
interest in *fabliau* stories, and in face of serious
opposition from the other adventure-seekers poor
Panurge no longer found his natural ingenuity a
source of the admiration for which his soul craved.
More remarkable still, whenever the author turns
to consider the lower manifestations of human nature,
—as he apparently did to stress serious contrasts with
affectations and unreality[1],—it is no longer ingenuity
but a true philosophical purpose[2] that drives him to
it. Even the friar, who in this respect had somewhat
degenerated to Panurge's level since Gargantuan days,
commented coldly upon Panurge's treatment of
Dindenault (*Q. L.* 8), and on another occasion told
a fabliau at the expense of the distracted doubter
who had turned to him for consolation. It is not that
Rabelais had lost interest in the old broadly funny
stories: he seems on the contrary to have thrown
himself wholeheartedly into the effective narration
of even the coarsest story[3]. But those which touch

[1] Cp. the tasks of the officers in Entelechie (*Quint Livre*, 22).
When his followers become querulous and disputative off
Chaneph, Pantagruel orders dinner (*Q. L.* 64).

[2] It must be remembered that Messer Gaster had supplanted
the ideal of feasting.

[3] It has been suggested above (Introd.) that Rabelais had to
yield to his readers' demand for more of the old matter, and that
he was turning to profit a former delight that no longer proved

upon subjects that in the previous period would have been legitimate spoils for Panurge and his fellows, came to be frowned upon by the nobler of the travellers. The story of the nun was disapproved by Pantagruel—a strange contrast with that of the 'haulte dame de Paris'—not on account of any pre-dilections in favour of orthodoxy but because the story seemed to touch upon *true* religion ('toute moinerie,' he said, 'craint moins les commandements de Dieu transgresser que leurs statutz provinciaulx'— *T. L.* 19). Nor is this an isolated instance. 'When you tell us such stories,' he later says (*Q. L.* 50), 'remember to have a basin brought. You almost make me sick. Using God's holy name in such filthy abominations!' And in spite of the great delight and spirit of the story of the Lord of Basché's treatment of the Chiquanous, in spite too of Pantagruel's hatred of all chicanery, most solemn thoughts rise to Pantagruel's lips and fierce indignation pours from Epistemon's[1]. Advancing age may have given him some distaste for such stories; artistic considerations may have had weight with him; but it is obvious that

so pleasant. In any case the expressions of disapproval are too frequent not to be sincere.

[1] 'Ceste narration, dist Pantagruel, sembleroit joyeuse, ne fust que devant nos œilz fault la crainte de Dieu continuellement avoir.—Meilleure, dist Epistemon, seroit, si la pluie de ces jeunes ganteletz fust sus le gras prieur tombée....Coups de poing eussent aptement atoure sa teste rase; attendue l'enorme con-cussion que voyons huy entre ces juges pedanées sous lorme. En quoy offensoient ces pauvres diables Chiquanoux?' *Q. L.* 16.

the critic of his own successful productions cannot
conceivably be of the same nature as the joyously
extravagant story-teller of the earlier books. To judge
from a wide comparison of materials in his later
romance, we might almost conclude that he had come
to realize that, however amusing a story may be to
the indifferent, to the victims the adventure would
have a very serious aspect. Probably this postulates
a spirit far too modern, but if *Pantagruel* had been
taken up to be refashioned after 1546 what could
Rabelais conceivably have made out of the adventures
which had charmed his readers and which had laid
their impress on his humour? *Gargantua* too contains those unsubstantial elements which the later
Rabelais could not help contrasting with real human
grossness and which would probably have been spoiled
by being adapted after that date. To us, however,—
whatever may have been the effect on his contemporaries,—the absence of the earlier comic element
is a gain rather than a loss, and the more so because
Rabelais came to exert certain subtle powers of
humour that are more in harmony with our
tastes.

Much of his humour throughout depends upon
ingenious play upon words and phrases. His mind
seems to have been of the type which readily absorbs
and uses proverbial expressions, or which, starting
with some such treasure of traditional wit, evolves

from it a whole legend or fantastic picture[1]. His early books swarm with common proverbs which in his later work were adapted to serious aims. Consequently it is not surprising that the *wine* of *Gargantua* and *Pantagruel* easily took on a figurative meaning (*A. P.*), or that the childish games of Gargantua—expressive of futile effort—came to be the serious pursuits of the Entelechian officers. Rabelais repeatedly took up phrases from his early work and applied them in a varied manner. He took them and *realized* them. Thus because there was a common saying that 'never was there such a marriage as that of the pear and cheese' ('encores dit on en nostre pays de vache quil ne fut onques tel mariage quest de la poire et du fromaige'), he enriched his story with the strange marriages of Ennasin. Because law apparitors were commonly said to thrive on blows, he made Friar John carry out his well-known experiment. Or alternatively he informed his readers that at Rome many people gain their *living* by *poisoning*, beating and killing; he wrote of spreading his quill to the wind; and he swore by the honour of a pedestrian. Such whimsical ingenuity may seem to recall the humour of the

---

[1] In *P.* p. 45 Panurge says: 'Je croy que lumbre de mon seigneur Pantagruel engendre les alterez, comme la lune faict les catarrhes,' and so (*P.* pp. 65–6) in the debate with Thaumaste we read: 'Et furent tant alterez de ceste seule voix quilz tiroyent la langue demy pied hors de la guele.' Note proverbial expressions in *G.* 5, 11, 32, many of which are turned to serious use in *Q. L.* 44, Prol. de l'Auteur, *Q. L.*, etc.

past[1], it reaches back, as we have seen, to the earliest pages of the romance, but the later serious use of such humorous matter must not pass without notice. The Ennasin episode includes references to marriage from covetous motives and other unnatural causes; the way in which the outraged Chiquanous went to work to blackmail and dun their unfortunate hasty-tempered victims is fully expounded; and at a time when the poor roads went in fear and trembling of the lurking robbers[2] the honour of a pedestrian might well be of much more weight than that of a cavalier. It is this serious element which saves such verbal ingenuities from becoming wearisome, but, seeing that they are mixed with many examples of a reversed process, they are liable to much misinterpretation.

For Rabelais' fertile invention was not likely to remain content with insinuating serious thoughts under a mocking appearance, and elsewhere—probably for prudential reasons,—it wilfully envelops earnest matter in the most ridiculous buffoonery. Rarely are his readers allowed to settle into a serious mood. If the thought becomes tense, if the author's purposes are in danger of being easily detected with

[1] In many *fabliaux* the point of the story depends upon the transparently arbitrary names, cp. Estula, Male Honte, etc.

[2] 'Les pauvres chemins craignoient les guetteurs de chemin et s'esloignoient d'eux comme des brigands,' *Quint Livre*, 26. Apparently the whole episode of the *Isle des Odes* came of a realization of commonplace phrases: 'Car les chemins cheminent comme animaux et sont les uns chemins errans...aultres, chemins passans, chemins croisans, chemins traversans,' etc.

consequent menace to himself, a quick turn of the action or a pseudo-learned display of evidence again plunges the story into the boisterously comic,—and thereby the effect of the seriousness is incidentally heightened. Pantagruel's denunciation of the Lord of Basché is strengthened by Friar John's experiment[1], and the prince's and Epistemon's gloomy meditations on death are enhanced by the Friar's vainglorious instance of his reckless prowess in defence of the Seuilly vines (*Q. L.* 23)[2]. Again, when the application of the obscure *Isle de Ruach* episode became somewhat plain, the author deliberately turned to consider the phenomenon of small rains beating down great winds (*Q. L.* 44). And when the Gaster episode promised to develop out of all proportion to his intention, even at the risk of alienating his readers' sympathy, he plunged them into the excellent chapter of nonsense in which he adduces 'evidence' that Gaster invented the means of turning back cannon balls in mid-air against the enemy[3]. Yet up to that point the episode had been a serious exposition of the importance of human needs, and the explanation of this and other examples is that no device was too absurd, no risk too great for him

[1] The Chiquanous threaten the Friar with judicial pursuit.
[2] A remarkable instance of Rabelais' later comments upon previous work. Cp. his later attitude to Thelema.
[3] This lengthy and very important episode is perhaps the most valuable indication that even when Rabelais felt strongly on any subject he could not resist his old impulse to discursive writing. See later.

to take rather than to allow his romance to appear earnest. The general unreality of it all forces the reader's mind to reflection, and from detection of the absurd to abstract the real sense. Bringuenarilles' ill-health arising out of consuming pots and pans instead of windmills provokes the recounting of strange deaths and this weighty speculation (in the author's mind) is dismissed with the commonplace statement that 'good Bringuenarilles died suffocated eating a little fresh butter by a warm stove, according to the doctor's orders[1].'

With all such beings who 'fly in the face of nature,' whose intellectual outlook is restricted in any way— but specially by metaphysical conceptions—and who fail to recognize the actual, there is grave danger that they may try to realize the imaginary. It was what the author of *Thelema* himself had done. It is what Don Quixote attempted. Now, not only is Rabelais' later romance full of such beings, but also in a certain definite sense the whole of it imposes upon the reader a feeling of the phantasmagoric in life. Rabelais conceived fantastic interludes, like the Andouilles, the Frozen Words, the Physeterre and Bringuenarilles, the most certain purpose of which appears to be to convince the reader that he is not in the everyday world but in a land of dreams which presents many

---

[1] Thus he combines his personal concern with the question of death, his hatred of oppressors like Bringuenarilles and satire of doctors. Cp. *G.* 23 for one of his medical principles.

points of resemblance to the actual world[1]. Some confusion arises from the procedure and the very common
use of metaphorical expressions and, still more, the
transformation of older literal expressions into figurative ways of speaking add to our difficulties. No longer
was the appearance of things, of the world, of man,
or even of man's language, accepted as being the
truth: Rabelais must try to get at the substance, and
his humour was turned to account in directing his
readers' attention to it. His interjection of protesta-
tions served the same purpose. Frequently, having
made some fantastic statement, he solemnly conjures
the reader to believe by asseverating that even the
travellers themselves could hardly believe what they
saw; at other times he plunges into the excitements
of a wild-goose chase, following with the utmost
recklessness the workings of his luxuriant imagination, until some preposterous phrase brings us back
to waking life[2]. The discussion of Andouillic importance in human life thus rambles on until Rabelais
wearies and adjures us to disbelieve it in its entirety,
when he has sufficiently misled the unthinking from
the real point. 'However,' he says, 'cease making
fools of yourselves now and believe that there's

---

[1] The early ideal was apparently to deck out the unreal and
impossible in realistic elements, a medieval *escape from life*
rather than a *criticism of life*. Cp. Swift's practice—whose
indebtedness to Rabelais was of the spirit.
[2] Rabelais was aware of this procedure at the time of the 1542
revision of *Pantagruel*, see note 1, p. 21.

nothing so true as the Gospel' ('Cessez pourtant icy plus vous trupher, et croyez quil nest rien si vray que l'Evangile,' *Q. L.* 38). With such good-humoured jesting at his reader's expense[1] Rabelais challenged us to detect his deceptions, or to turn from what is obviously nonsense to what experience may interpret, and the practical effect is to make the victim read in future with the greater care.

It is therefore to be expected that the later Rabelais delighted in caricaturing human beings, in selecting that idea or passion which, being over-developed, marks the man. In the later romance grotesque figures swarm; and it has been too often assumed that Rabelais' typical creations are the monsters of the *Quint Livre*. It is not so: his mature characters are much more subtle, even the realistic being suggestively sketched with this truth in view. Thus Panurge, who never quite banished from his mind the idea that his marriage must end in disaster, interprets the sound of church bells as 'marie poinct, marie poinct' or 'marie toy, marie toy' according to his mood, and, in the performance of duties for which he was quite unfitted, Bridoye, resorting to dice, becomes a perfect automaton. It is undoubtedly a general human fault that a consuming passion forces the individual to adopt unconsciously certain actions and expressions. The birds of the *Isle Sonante* fell

---

[1] This is the charm of many modern humorists, cp. *Tristram Shandy*.

completely under the control of bells; the 'janspill'-hommes' (Prol. de l'Auteur, *Q. L.*), blindly imitating the poor woodcutter, bring upon themselves a deserved fate; Grippeminauld, with all his terrors, has fallen into uttering 'Or ça,' a phrase which alone makes him human; nay Jupiter himself, through having dispensed justice to mankind in all their concerns, becomes indeed the servant, and not the master, of his creation, with the result that he appears distracted at moments of terrestrial excitement[1]. The most explicit example of this kind of humour, however, is to be found in the later satire of monks, for, although one of the travellers diverts us by adducing proofs of the mysterious powers resident in kitchen utensils, the author there assures us that the true force impelling monks kitchenwards exists in the monkish mind itself (*Q. L.* 11). Like men of all professions, they tend to think in terms of their special interests, and so they cannot imagine anything apart from food and drink. The most comic of Rabelais' professional men use jargon both relevantly and otherwise. The philosopher, skilled in the exercises of the schools and practising the philosophic calm of an unconcerned spectator, is confronted with a painfully earnest and perplexed Panurge; and Trouillogan's nonchalance passes readily into the ways of speech of an experienced academic debater. Thenceforth all

[1] Even so he refuses to decide in the Ramus-Galland controversy.

that Panurge's ingenuity can extract from him is 'il
y a de l'apparence,' or 'pour cause,' or 'possible est,'
or 'il n'est pas impossible,' or 'il est vraysemblable'
(*T. L.* 36); and we feel that in this humorous touch
Rabelais has conveyed a more incisive satire than in
all the obscene and coarse ridicule of *Pantagruel.* In
this remarkable scene we cannot help feeling with
what childish glee the devotee to abstract terms and
disinterested speculations triumphs over the realists
with whom he conferred. It is still Rabelais' pro-
foundest conviction, his realism, that gives point to
his mature humour; but, since the marriage question
had probably been a really personal one with Rabelais,
this association of the comic Trouillogan with a
serious interest makes the realism more notable. The
philosopher is in a sense a more noteworthy creation
than the theologian Homenas. Yet, if we bear in
mind the temptation of superficially religious folk[1]
to fall into the habit of uttering meaningless stereo-
typed phrases, the latter is a powerful figure, sug-
gestive of Rabelais' observation and even of his
religious development. When the travellers fall into
the old decretalist's humour with all manner of
anecdotes relating to the power of the decretals (many
of them unquotable), Homenas acclaims each one
joyfully with 'vengeance et punition divine,' or
'miracle, miracle, miracle' (*Q. L.* 52), in a manner
which suggests that, however estimable the man may

[1] *Or* hypocrites, like Tartuffe.

be, his character is marred by narrowness of view. And what is most significant is that the humour of the Trouillogan and Homenas episodes is comparatively genial[1] though the satire is even more powerful than that of the story of Bragmardo (*G.* 18–20). It demands in the author a profounder knowledge of humanity, presupposes in him a firmer grasp of reality, so firm indeed as almost to exclude supramundane interests; and it demands in the readers co-operation with the author in the attainment of his purpose, since they must themselves discover the weakness of the character. And just as it is we who carry out the satiric intention, so it is in part we who, on a short view, infer that Rabelais did exclude the higher life from his thoughts. Indeed, in comparison with the humour of his early work, that of the last three books rather demonstrates the reverse to be the truth.

When all things are considered, under the play of the imagination the most undoubted water may taste like delicious wine of various kinds according to the individual's fancy[2], and within limits the effects of imaginative powers justify their exercise. But being quite unrestrained the imagination of Homenas and

---

[1] The mature Rabelais laughs at vices rather than at men. After all, Panurge had rejected Trouillogan's commonsense advice, which resembles Pantagruel's, and so Trouillogan becomes comic only in regard to his one defect; likewise Homenas, apart from his obsession, is represented as genial and hospitable.

[2] *Quint Livre*, 43.

of the lady of Entelechie leads to their downfall. Just
as the priest, obsessed with the decretals, can foreshadow an earthly paradise following upon the universal study of them, so the Queen of Quinte Essence
lives in a world that she has imagined, does everything that is impossible and cures all the incurables.
The charming, sympathetic and womanly figure lives
on in our minds, marred only by the false learning
which prevented her from judging the world on
its merits. Her sincere but extraordinary welcome
abashed even the ready-witted Panurge[1] and imposed
silence upon the company, and that fact alone enabled
her to trace their descent from the Pythagorean
school of philosophers and to express heart-felt sympathy with them in the perplexities they must have
experienced at the outset ('En ceste vostre taciturnite
cognoy je que non seulement estes issus de l'escole
Pythagorique, de laquelle print racine en successive
propagation l'antiquite de mes progeniteurs, mais aussi
qu'en Egypte, célèbre officine de haute philosophie,
mainte lune retrograde vos ongles mordus avez, et la
teste d'un doigt grattée,' *Quint Livre*, 20). Perhaps
this picture of the lady of Entelechie is the best reply
to the charge that Rabelais was and remained the
enemy of woman. Not even Molière,—though the
demands of the stage prevented his doing otherwise
than he did,—succeeded in portraying the 'femme

[1] There is a remarkable contrast between the Panurge here,
and the earlier one who fell in love with the 'haulte dame.'

savante' with such delicacy, or in turning our laughter upon the false learning and inappropriateness of citation, which are the distinguishing features of the type. From his gross, coarse and often incredible ridicule of his early opponents Rabelais had developed enormously. No longer directed at men and women, in whom among fine qualities there may be grievous faults, but at the faults themselves, Rabelais' laughter had become gentle, though powerful; it had become humane and modern.

In the period subsequent to 1546, as we have seen, Rabelais' humour, though varied, appears to spring from the healthy stock of reality. Critics have commonly accepted that it had always so originated. There is, however, a difference. He came to laugh at everything that was commonly accepted in place of the actual, whereas before that date, taking his stand on lower levels, he had mocked at everything which was not ideal and at every man who did not represent the Renaissance. The change must have come about through his gaining a profounder knowledge of life and of the springs of human conduct. To convince himself that he need not create the exaggerated, he must have detected among his fellows the almost universal lack of moderation, and then have sought instances of it in real life. And since man is prone to laugh at excesses from which he is, or believes that he is, himself free, at extravagance only if he holds moderate and definite views, and at social excess only if he is unmoved by the spirit of a partisan, we must conclude that the old ardent 'Reformist' student had undergone some process of transformation. Humour reveals the man, and it seems clear that Rabelais must obviously have changed. By a comparison of the subject-matter in the early and the later books we may be able to trace the new position that he had taken up.

3. CHANGES IN CHARACTERIZATION

W^E may legitimately conclude from the fore-going examination of Rabelais' humour that the most remarkable developments in characterization may be expected. As we understand the term to-day this narrative power demands that the author's personality shall be so projected into his creations that his work shall produce an illusion of reality and that the actions of his characters shall appear to be *their* reactions to *their* surroundings. This would seem to demand further a great sympathy with the author's fellows, such as, in fact, developed in Rabelais.

Consistently followed up, even the machinery of giants might result—in spite of obvious difficulties—in a coherent story with actual gigantic character development and with gigantic personalities acting upon others and being reacted upon. In point of fact, however, Rabelais did not even maintain the giant-quality; even in the first two books he had to return to it, and later he appears almost to have let it fall into oblivion. The diversion of his readers and himself with *Pantagruel*, and the polemic of *Gargantua*, made character studies superfluous, and, since the intrusion of his personal opinions was the essence of the polemic, probably impossible. We must concede that he seems to have been aware of the need for something of the kind, if only because he confronted Gargantua with Picrochole and Pantagruel with Loupgarou, but this traditional trick of contrasting embodied virtues and vices is wearisome judged by modern standards. Those beings lack fine observation, and, gaining in clear definition, they lack reality. His most successful creations in the early books, Panurge and Friar John, were however so much alive that they but partly served their creator's purposes[1], and so prominent a place did they claim that they must have revealed the essential weakness of the other characters. The monstrous Pantagruel of 1532 in no sense derives from the bourgeois Gargantua, and this might be expected if the latter conception, as seems almost certain, sprang from Rabelais' visit to the Touraine in 1534. Grandgousier and Gargantua, it has been suggested, are half portraits of Rabelais' grandfather and father[2], and it may be that at the time of the composition of *Gargantua* the three giants were to represent three generations of his family. They would still serve Rabelais' purpose in that the naïveté of the older times would reveal the true glory of his own[3], and so would exalt

[1] Friar John rejected Ponocrates' rules for drinking and ridiculed the idea of study for monks, surely two fairly important principles in Rabelais' eyes. He and Panurge represent reality breaking in upon the didactic conceptions. Contradictions abound in the two books, however, cp. Grandgousier on the plague (*G.* 45) with passage quoted above, p. 11, n. 1, etc.

[2] *R.E.R.* 1908, pp. 38 and 265. For differences between the giants see Lefranc, Introduction to *Gargantua*, p. lxxvii.

[3] Gargantua, in his letter to Pantagruel (*P.* pp. 25–6), points out the superiority of the modern to the past age.

the present at the expense of the past. Even so they would mark an advance upon the notions of the earlier book for, though Gargantua embodied generosity and Picrochole rapacity, they are not so described, whereas in *Pantagruel* the persons were labelled with the qualities they stood for[1]. With all his superficiality and simplicity Gargantua never fell to so low a level as Pantagruel, Epistemon and Panurge did in the scene where respectively they uttered knightly, gluttonous and sensual comments upon a suggested idea[2]. Certainly apart from Friar John and Panurge the characters of the first two books did not distract attention from the adventures, and it might be maintained that Panurge was merely the occasion of the narratives which group round him, and that Friar John served to introduce the well-told story of the struggle at Seuilly. It appears more probable however that they too, besides Gargantua and his father, were painted from the life. Certainly in so far as they are real persons, they and only they showed indications of Rabelais' approaching mastery.

Friar John is the simpler and more uniform of the two greater creations. From the first to last he delights in all manner of activity. According to his own state-

[1] Eusthenes, Epistemon, Panurge and Carpalim describe themselves (*P.* p. 80). Panurge (πανοῦργος) appears as the bold one though he seems to have owed much to the *Miles gloriosus* of Latin and somewhat to the Pharmakos of Greek comedy.

[2] Contrast the much later scene (*Q. L.* 22–3) where, though each expresses his personal views on death, it is the noblest which stands forth prominent.

ment (*G.* 40) he had spent the greater part of his life in field sports and in the preparation of snares and gins; and in view of his most notable deed, the defence of Seuilly vineyard, we may legitimately doubt whether Gargantua's panegyric is quite deserved. The friar is an excellent companion at table, given up wholly to good living (*G.* 39), but it is doubtful whether he cared sufficiently about the afflicted and distressed to defend them[1]. His impetuosity is as clear from the account of the attack on Seuilly as in the frequent offers to go and sack the lurking places of monsters[2]. He cares equally little for the devils whom Panurge fears in Raminagrobis' chamber, but the reason is not so much bravery (though his unshaken courage during the storm shows up well against the behaviour of his cowardly companion), as the cynical views that he held with reference to religion and religious folk. And his cynicism is that of the simple: he has apparently lived in the monastery so long that he is in all respects ill at ease in the great world. He is utterly unworldly, refusing Touquedillon's ransom because he cares nothing for money (*G.* 46), and when the king pays the money on behalf of his prisoner, returning it to the royal war chest. He is quite unprepared to accept the government of the

[1] Indeed defending the abbey vineyard is the climax of Gargantua's speech (*G.* 40).

[2] Quaresmeprenant, the robbers of Ganabin and Grippeminauld. Note too his outspoken denunciation of the cowardly disciples and the fugitives of Pavia (*G.* 39).

prospective monastery because he feels that a man
who cannot govern himself cannot govern others
(*G.* 52), and later, apart from his breviary in which
he seems to place the greatest trust, he turns helplessly to Pantagruel for guidance. Among the serious
problems of life the friar, who had scornfully rejected
the proferred interpretation of the Thelema enigma,
was utterly helpless. He had scorned learning (*G.* 39),
had wondered at his companions being pricked with
the desire to learn, and when the old Macrobe had
expounded his views on the fates of heroes after
death he was unable to accept them ('Ces heros icy
et semidieux desquelz avez parlé peuvent ilz par mort
finir? Par nettre dene, je pensois en pensarois quilz
fussent immortelz comme beaux anges, Dieu me le
veuille pardonner. Mais ce reverendissime Macrobe dit
quilz meurent finablement,' *Q. L.* 27). Yet apart from
his touching confidence in Pantagruel's opinion in
the later books Friar John did not develop except
perhaps in taking over much of Panurge's grossness,
and even that is uncertain. On his first introduction
(in *Gargantua*) he did not meet Panurge, but in
almost every sense except delight in the grossness
which so deeply offended Pantagruel he is the anti-
thesis of the really central character of the romance.
In courage and rash physical enterprise he is vastly
superior to Panurge, and at least once we are glad
that the friar could delight in *fabliaux* if only because
he could so completely mock a foolish Panurge.

It may be that Friar John remained constant because he was a picture of the author himself; it may be that the Panurge of *Pantagruel* was another aspect of the same individual; but such suggestions are beside the point. We can hardly doubt that Rabelais did not lack materials for depicting the needy adventurer, wandering from place to place and diverting by his bragging and ingenuity[1]. We cannot hesitate to believe that the author's life had introduced him to many such beings who were the heroes of somewhat dubious exploits. What is of supreme importance is that later the braggart Panurge, whose own description showed his boldness[2], was selected to display the most abject cowardice in danger, and the most comical perplexity on a moral question that Rabelais himself had settled[3]. The early Panurge was a man of action; it is not too much to say that in the later work Rabelais made a psychological study of him, and—in view of the fact that the old self-seeker actually aspired to 'put aside all human affections,' as he was advised (*T. L.* 13)—that the creator was

---

[1] Apart from Plautus' *Miles gloriosus* to whom for Panurge and Pantagruel as at first sketched he was perhaps indebted.

[2] 'Moy dist Panurge, jentreprens de entrer en leur camp par le milieu des gardes et du guet, et banqueter avec eulx a leurs despens, sans estre congneu de nully, et de visiter lartillerie, et aussi visiter les tentes de tous les capitaines, et me prelasser par les bandes sans iamais estre descouvert' (*P.* p. 80).

[3] There seems to be little doubt that Rabelais had 'married' before *T. L.* appeared. Dolet mentions his little son's death.

inclined to mock his creature[1]. Indeed the *Tiers Livre* seems to be mainly intended to ridicule Panurge and his various researches. Contemporaries at all events would rarely need guidance in perceiving their absurdity, since, at a time when most men could recall from experience similar consultations ending in similar disillusionment, the gravity with which the various sources of wisdom were consulted and the helpless credulity of the enquirer until some notion threw him back upon his haunting dread or until the advice baffled him, must have been more vividly incongruous than in our days[2]. And in themselves the adventures did not demand a powerful sense of humour, nor even great speculative boldness. The visit to a witch, for instance, did not affect Epistemon in the least, and as a preliminary Pantagruel had discussed it with the utmost firm reasonableness. Indeed the prince's habitual dissuasion and his depreciation of most of the consultations may appear as a serious flaw in the book. But in the case of Her Trippa even that was unnecessary: Panurge himself told a story

[1] Cp. the Storm episode and specially *Q. L.* 23, which opens with Panurge saying: 'Ha ha tout va bien,' etc. and closes with Panurge's reply to the sailor who assures him that the ship's timbers are still two inches thick, 'Et ne crains rien que les dangiers.' At sight of the Physeterre he cries for Perseus.

[2] Rabelais had always been sceptical of divination, cp. *P.* p. 27: 'laisse moy lastrologie divinatrice, et lart de Lullius comme abuz et vanitez'; also the *Pantagrueline Prognostications*.

discreditable to that person's pretensions[1]. Like Her Trippa, Tiresias was represented as qualifying his prophecies with 'ce que je diray adviendra ou n'adviendra poinct' (*T. L.* 22)[2]. In spite of all Panurge continued his quest which would at least serve the purpose of warding off his thoughts by allowing him to indulge in some activity. We may dimly see the reception of this book in which, while the old jovial laugh excited by Panurge's tricks was rarely provoked, the sapping of age-old beliefs would conjure up a smile in men who were not positively sceptical. In a measure laughter alienates the laugher from his victim, and the provocation of laughter at the older hero's expense was a dangerous proceeding. The readers of *Pantagruel* must have been cruelly deceived in their expectations, and both Epistemon and Friar John therefore gave their private opinions of their comrade. The one adjured him to take medical advice and discussed patronizingly with him various divinatory methods (though he sternly declined to accompany him on an extravagant journey to consult an oracle—*T. L.* 24), and the other gave his advice in the form of a *fabliau* which though turned against himself the old Panurge would have enjoyed.

[1] Her Trippa practised some of the arts upon which Thaumaste came to consult Pantagruel. He needed no such powers, however, and foretold Panurge's fate from his appearance, offering confirmation only by his arts.

[2] The author adds: 'Et est le style des prudens prognostiqueurs.'

These two interviews assured the readers that it was their old hero who had changed, that perhaps he was abnormal, and that at any rate his fellows were superior to him, and consequently that they might laugh at him in safety; as it was intended that they should.

Nonetheless he was the same being as they had already known, habitually satisfying the needs of the moment in his restlessly active career. The only difference was that he was forced to reflect on realizing his desire for the more social amenities of married life. The fixed idea that his marriage would turn out ill[1],—derived no doubt from his former adventures,—dominated his mind, held up all constructive action and penetrated his being through and through. His first consultation with his master would alone suffice to reveal his impotence of will. From his own mouth however we hear of his dependence upon all external influences[2]. 'I wish nothing but what you advise me,' he cries to Trouillogan, and this, properly considered, is in full agreement with his character in *Pantagruel*, though no longer was he intended to be the admiration of his former

[1] Although at every suggestion of a new quest to be made he appears optimistic, yet the slightest difficulty and still more the slightest ill-omen provokes his fears. The various quests afford him an outlet for his activity.

[2] He echoes Pantagruel's desire for knowledge, when with certain information that Her Trippa is not infallible, he yields to Epistemon with 'Bien, allons vers luy....On ne scauroit trop apprendre' (*T. L.* 25).

admirers. Toleration of the quips and tricks of an ingenious vagrant and idle amusement at them are possible to most human beings because in a greater or less degree humanity partakes of his turbulent nature, but certainly a much higher form of amusement, because provocative of reflection, is possible if circumstances convert him into an aspirant to social honours and privileges. Panurge's picture of himself as a father is almost pathetic; he even promises to practise good husbandry though he lacks the power to initiate personal reforms. Now the advice repeatedly given to him insists upon the personal exertion of choice, and the resultant situation suggests that the author had developed a totally new attitude towards humanity[1]. He had analyzed human nature and resynthesized it with the new elements derived from his reflection. The transformation in Panurge is admirably touched upon when later the prospect of even greater freedom than his journeys to oracles and witches had allowed, and of adventurous activity in which he may forget his mental embarassments, opens before him (*T. L.* 47). The old carefree Panurge comes again to the fore. He readily promises absolute fidelity to his chief. He gloats over the marvels they are to behold. He is prepared, he says, relying upon his old ingenuity, to face all dangers; and he attributes to his indulgent patron his own

[1] Cp. the arresting fact that in *P.* Panurge's adventures had been largely anti-social.

taste for aimless vagabondage, hailing him as an 'amateur de peregrinite[1].'

When we consider what Rabelais had made of the old Panurge, we can but wonder that he left Friar John almost undeveloped. It may be that that splendid figure of a very successful book remained constant because he was an unreflecting man of action in whom the author became less and less interested. Certainly the companions debate and dispute with one another, and although Panurge became the general butt for their ridicule (for whom they feel a kind of affectionate regard) we are made to feel that the author had advanced to being critical of most of their fancies and ideas. He seems to be almost wholly concerned with thinkers and their opinions,—whence one great difficulty in interpreting the later work,—whereas earlier he had been interested in actions and the advocacy of certain cherished ideals. But perhaps there is another and a better explanation, more in agreement with his previous ambitions. His later characterization may be an improvement upon the earlier crude attempt to depict the glory of the Renaissance in contrast with the preceding ages.

All Panurge's deeds had resembled those of the *fabliaux*. He was a being who had escaped from the

[1] In the same way Panurge says of Her Trippa (*T. L.* 25): 'Il ne scait le premier traict de philosophie, qui est Cognois toy.' This is the gravest fault of Panurge himself. When danger threatens, Panurge is the first to suggest the renunciation of his quest.

pages of such collections of stories, and in a more daringly speculative epoch he naturally found himself bewildered. He believes unquestioningly in the supernatural and correspondingly disbelieves human and scientific evidence. Doctors, theologians and lawyers all seem to him far inferior to the witch, and yet in spite of all his zeal for supernatural mystery his visit to the Sibyl of Panzouste reveals him as terrified and 'Epistemon scornful of a realistic scene of charlatanry (*T. L.* 16–17). In Raminagrobis' death-chamber (*T. L.* 22) he fears devils of whom he professes full and certain knowledge[1], while the friar, his companion, is unimaginatively or callously fearless. The rencounter with a shipload of monks fills him alone with joy[2], and, most notable instance of all, while the others yearn and strive to investigate the mystery of the Frozen Words, Panurge cowers in terror before something that he cannot understand[3]. Yet he cannot accept Hippothadée's assurance on the question of marriage, because with regard to woman as in everything else the past traditional views cling round him. Consequently he stands aloof, separated from the humblest of his com-

[1] Cp. his explanation of the 'diabolology of Toledo' (*T. L.* 23) which he had studied.

[2] In spite of Erasmus' use of the common saying. Note also how severely he attacks Raminagrobis' mockery of the friars, and his reproofs of Friar John in the Storm.

[3] This scene contains a remarkable clash of personalities which Rabelais could not possibly have so briefly represented had he not profoundly studied man.

panions by the widest of gulfs. Panurge accepts those
discreditable stories as a store of wisdom on woman's
ways and the dangers of marriage, while to the others
they appear rather as a store of easy amusements.
His jealousy betrays a primitive organism which in
its fear of an invasion of its rights will alternately
indulge in wildest sentimentalism and in plans for a
brutal and savage vengeance. He is an egocentric,
as he had always been. Indeed he is not peculiar
in that respect in the romance, but for similar
examples we must turn back to Grandgousier and
Gargantua who had entered the married state only
for their personal comfort and convenience, unless
indeed they had done so because society demanded it.
We have seen that there is reason to believe that the
giants represented the past, and we must conclude
that in the author's eyes Panurge became the embodiment of what was not modern, of all that was dead
and an encumbrance on humanity. His cowardice,
his vacillating purpose, and his readiness to renounce
his quest,—like his dreams of dolphins that shall
carry his will to its destination, though the existence
of heirs remains doubtful,—all betoken the old non-
practical medieval mind, which had always before
been *hated* by Rabelais and was now to be laughed
at. In vain may Panurge's advocacy of moderation
be adduced in proof of his character being somewhat
akin to the author's own, for a comparison of his
sermon to Dindenault and Rabelais' advocacy of

moderation elsewhere will show clearly how medieval
in tone Panurge's easy philosophy was. Dindenault
must demand no more than a fair price for his sheep[1]
simply because in history there had been cases of
poetic justice. The central figure of the story appears
still to believe in the justice of the older allegorists,
while Rabelais had insisted that man's demand for
'justice' in this world was in itself a proof of human
presumption and unworthiness (Prol. *Q. L.*). It will
therefore appear probable that, retaining his great
creation, the author had adopted altogether different
views of him. In Panurge Rabelais may have portrayed a common type of contemporary by whom he
had been formerly amused, and consequently he in-
vited the old admirers to examine what the real
Panurge stood for and to criticize themselves in the
light of nobler and the noblest characters. But what
self-examination as well as study of others would not
this development postulate! It must be so, however,
for both in Epistemon and still more in Pantagruel
do we find personalities immeasurably superior, be-

---

[1] 'Advisez que ne soit trop,' he says, 'vous nestes le premier
de ma cognoissance qui, trop tost voulant riche devenir et
parvenir, est a lenvers tombe en pauvrete voire quelquefois sest
romper le col' (*Q. L.* 7). (Is it an allusion to Judas Iscariot?)
In the Prologue the author uses the acquisition of wealth to
inculcate other principles, but in *P.* he delighted in the prospect
of 'great lords getting a miserable living in Hell, while philosophers and those who had been poor in this world were in their
turn great lords' (*P.* p. 100). Rabelais' later work shows him
realizing that but too frequently in this world the evil flourished.

cause more modern, to the superstitious Panurge and the active Friar John.

Like the remaining characters in *Pantagruel*, Epistemon proclaims his special faculty for warlike duties; and he forthwith outlines the character that he will later have. With one exception, however. Not only is he cognizant of stratagems and prowess from the study of the worthy captains of the past, of all their tricks and cunning, but also he himself can put that cunning into practice[1]. The opportunity for a display of his cunning occurs both in that book and in the *Quart Livre*, but his failure to display his powers later must not be attributed to braggart propensities for usually he is as good as his word. He is the pedantic tutor of Pantagruel (*P*. p. 18) and his main duty,—apart from acting as *corpus vile* for Panurge to restore from the dead (*P*. pp. 97–8),—was to acquire vast stores of learning from the ancients. His acquisitions stand him and his fellows in good stead in the *Tiers Livre* for it is he who marshals the authorities in support of the various methods of divination, and in so doing he is often called upon to oppose authority to authority. He quotes the Law of Moses against having resort to a witch as well as

---

[1] 'Moy, dist Epistemon, je scay tous les stratagemates et prouesses des vaillans capitaines et champions du temps passe, et toutes les ruses et finesses de discipline militaire, je yray, et encores que feusse descouvert et descele, je eschapperay en leur faisant croire de vous tout ce quil me plaira: car je suis de la lignee de Sinon' (*P*. p. 80.)

the belief of ancient Platonists on the Genius (who-
ever may see his Genius can foretell the future,
T. L. 24). But after the *Tiers Livre*, his peculiar
task being completed, he falls into the background,
and except for his courageous behaviour in the great
storm (out of which he comes with hands torn by
ropes), and his speculation that man's destiny lies
'partly in the will of God and partly in his own
discretion,' he plays no part, unless it be to confirm
Pantagruel's opinions. He was a stupendously learned
man, who, wholly engrossed in his researches, was
thereby unable to come to a decision unless his
beloved classical authorities gave him clear guidance.
Pantagruel found it necessary to oppose Epistemon
on several points, and therefore we must infer that
it is to that character, who takes up in the last two
books Epistemon's abandoned task, that we must
look for Rabelais' final hero and ideal.

Quite early in the *Tiers Livre* Pantagruel showed
that traditional beliefs weighed lightly upon him[1].
He will tolerate no restriction of enquiry and his later
utterances show that he will accept authoritative
utterances only when his observation and his reflection confirm them. Thus he warns the company
that, in spite of the extraordinary mass of evidence
in support of Vergilian lots, experience has proved
the absolute unreliability of that method (*T. L.* 10);
and he speaks with utter contempt of resort to oracles

[1] *T. L.* 16. Contrast the earlier Pantagruel, see pp. 24–5.

who, he says, deceive by involved and meaningless speech (*T. L.* 19). It seems indeed that the others are aware that he disapproves of many enquiries that the credulous Panurge makes: 'Let us go back to our King,' says Panurge, 'I am certain that he will be displeased with us if he happens to hear that we have been into the lair of this befrocked devil' (*T. L.* 25). And his superiority is not only one of rank. He is in fact treated by his suite as a nobler fellow-seeker after truth rather than as the master of their fortunes. In various discussions his opinion met with opposition, but with opposition much more reasonable and deliberate than Friar John's rejection of his master's interpretation of the Enigma. But whereas in the earlier book the prince advances a conventional and the commoner a novel explanation, the rôles in later books are reversed. It is Pantagruel himself who, athirst for knowledge, utters the most refreshing and daring speculations. Besides, whereas the young prince is applauded for his judgment between two claimants (*P.* pp. 32–44), he merely gives humane advice in the case of Bridoye and comments upon the case as a spectator (*T. L.* 43), and yet later before Grippeminauld receives equal treatment with his companions. Indeed he seems more abashed by that monster than they. Now it is true that in the first case he was in his father's country and abroad in the later cases, but that does not explain the difference: no such refinements may be expected of Rabelais. It may rather be argued that Pantagruel speaks out the strongest convictions of Rabelais' mature mind, *or* perhaps those opinions which he had most admired. In his part, it may be, we ought to seek for the central thought necessary to the story and to our understanding of Rabelais' philosophy. When he falls asleep *over a book of fiction* the interest of all slackens (*Q. L.* 63) and the other travellers seek to beguile their tedium in various idle ways; and although in the Storm scene we are interested in Friar John's activity and amused by Panurge's terror, we never lose sight of the quiet dignified leader whose place is at the helm (*Q. L.* 19). Elsewhere he guides and controls their deliberations. He acts as the experienced, learned, and benevolent counsellor of Panurge in the *Tiers Livre*, except in the more ridiculous consultations. He hovers in the background, on occasion coming forward with suggestions and explanations, and with some pregnant reflection or expressive gesture he directs opinion and outlines the sympathetic personality of a great man.

With all that his figure remains vague. Unlike Panurge, he was a man whom Rabelais did not fully understand. There were elements in his character with which he could sympathize no doubt and which he could admire, and yet substantially the portrait remained, like Thelema, an abstraction to the end. Panurge, we have seen, probably represented the past, possibly may have depicted the earlier Rabelais whose hero he had been, and certainly he had become inferior to Rabelais who only then could laugh at him; Pantagruel's character changes similarly, it is true, but whether on account of his rank[1] or of his personal qualities he was always as superior to the author as Panurge became inferior. In the *Tiers Livre* two almost irreconcilable descriptions are given, but while the one ('cestoit le meilleur petit et grand bon hommet que onques ceignit espee,' *T. L.* 2) is found in what is generally admitted to be work of the earlier period (*T. L.* 1–8), the second represents Trinquamelle's profound respect for the great judgment, good sense and sound learning with which the prince was naturally endowed (*T. L.* 43). This improvement may be explainable as due to a growing and incomplete appreciation of true greatness which would make of Pantagruel a less convincing figure than Panurge. Nevertheless we get sufficient glimpses of the noble creation's thought to be able to outline what had impressed Rabelais. The prince urged the control of personal whims by custom, though in other contexts he pleaded for greater individual freedom. 'Everybody,' he says, 'has a right to his own opinion,

---

[1] In composing *Pantagruel* the author claimed to have served the hero ('le quel jay servy a gaiges des ce que je fuz hors de paige, jusques a present,' *P.* p. 5). Both the early books were revised for a new edition in 1542, and such a fact was likely to be turned to real purpose. To picture his personal patron as the mature Pantagruel would necessitate a vital change and be in agreement with Rabelais' realism.

even in external and impartial matters, and such opinions are neither good nor evil because they do not come from our hearts and our thoughts, the seat of all that is good or evil. They are good if our affections are good and controlled by a clean mind; they are evil if our affections are wickedly depraved by the evil one. Only I personally dislike novelty and neglect of custom' (*T. L.* 7). On this ground he will honour an individual's convictions, but he will insist on his own convictions being respected. He maintains that the question of marriage is a personal one, to be decided by each man for himself[1], though he has not the least doubt on it (*T. L.* 48) but thinks maybe that we should consider it from a social point of view (*T. L.* 35). Under no circumstances, he there urged, must man neglect his social activities and duties through the poltroonery of taking jealous care of his spouse, and in this as in connection with the work of the doctor, the lawyer and the theologian he had decided that men must detach themselves from inherited prejudice and take a wider view of human affairs (*T. L.* 29). Nevertheless he could

[1] *T. L.* 29. On the subject of Raminagrobis' answer he says to Panurge: 'En l'entreprinse de mariage chascun doibt estre arbitre de ses propres pensees et de soy mesme conseil prendre. Telle a tousjours este mon opinion, et autant vous en dis la premiere fois que men parlastes. Mais vous en mocquiez tacitement.' In face of such utterances it appears impossible to maintain that the *Tiers Livre* is wholly a contribution to the *Querelle des Femmes*, or that it treats of marriage for three-quarters of its length.

tolerate the most irritating irresolution in Panurge[1], and his practice, coupled with his views, qualified him as the guide through the perplexities of their voyage. He denounced false learning as powerfully as Rabelais' prologues do. He showed cause why we should doubt the sufficiency of the human reason (*T. L.* 44). He preserved a calm faith in things that were for the time impossible of demonstration (*Q. L.* 63). He could not bring himself to disregard the deeper human feelings, and the death of Pan affected him to tears. He had discovered within himself powers transcending reason, only to be compared with the δαίμων of Socrates. It will thus be seen that his chief quality is the devouring desire to explore the knowable. This his father recognized when he reluctantly consented to his undertaking the journey to the Oracle (*T. L.* 48), but the truth that Pantagruel sought was not the truth as to marriage; it was not to be found in learning; nor was it abstract truth; it was the truth of human nature, of human beliefs and of human destiny.

Pantagruel is then an exalted new kind of man. We can hardly doubt which, of Pantagruel or Panurge, will give utterance to Rabelais' thought. Rejection of traditional behaviour, recognition of the limits of reason and careful discrimination between facts in the light of reality and humanity are fresh

---

[1] Of whom, he asks, 'N'estes vous asceuré de vostre vouloir?' (*T. L.* 10).

ideals or purposes distinct from the encyclopaedic
learning with which Rabelais had formerly identified
himself. Whence then had the realistic Rabelais
obtained material for this sketch of his ideal man?
It is quite possible that an acute observer of life,
as he is proved to have been, could by considerable
reflection have built up this noble conception. There
are indeed elements in his early life and character, as
revealed in his writings and in his actions, which might
have constituted an ever-growing ideal personage;
and it is perhaps rather by activity than by thought or
reading that an individual's personality both displays
itself and is modified. Rabelais himself had defied
ecclesiastical authority and public opinion by deserting
the monastery for medicine and anatomy; he had
been urged on by his feeling for reality; and he had
horrified admiring friends by his turn for daring
speculation. As will be seen later, his active life had
apparently led him to adopt a critical attitude towards
his learning and his old principles. Still this theory
does not appear to be wholly in harmony with
Rabelais' previous literary practice; he had always
drawn his most convincing figures—Gargantua,
Grandgousier and probably Friar John and Panurge
—from the life; and it is hardly to be expected that,
having once discovered this secret, he should not still
do so. It is therefore possible that Guillaume du
Bellay's personality had contributed much to the
splendid Pantagruel. The later books are, indeed,

full of pathetic references to his great patron. He, like Pantagruel, had steadily turned his face from miraculous explanations of phenomena, he had treated questions of war and religion on broad statesmanlike grounds uninfluenced by creed, and not only was he the noblest man of Rabelais' circle but even possibly the most truly enlightened man of his time[1].

[1] Guillaume du Bellay was a man of Rabelais' own age (*b.* 1491, *d.* 1542). Primarily a diplomat, he was forced by circumstances into opposition to the Catholic hierarchy as it fell more and more under the Emperor's power. He used his influence with the French Universities, and with his brother, Jean du Bellay (who later took Rabelais to the court of the liberal and reformist Paul III), in support of Henry VIII's divorce; and in his frequent visits to Protestant and Catholic German princes he had to subordinate *in practice* his religious beliefs, which his memoirs show to have been sincere, to the more urgent political (national) needs. His controlling motive was service to France, and he excelled in reconciling quarrelsome chiefs, lifting the personal question to this nobler level (*Mém.* III. 397 ff.): his reasoned moderation is finely displayed in his letter to the German States (IV. 30 ff.) consequent upon the murder of two ambassadors by Spanish agents: 'Qui une fois a passé les bornes de honte, il fault que tost après il devienne apertement et naïvement impudent,' and the same philosophic justification of action urged him to oppose the proposed war with reasons that bear upon the country's need for peace, trade and rest. True, this reasoning was overborne, but only by the reflection that before all such considerations of prosperity, it was essential to protect the humblest French subjects on Spanish soil. Like Grandgousier, he showed in his government of Turin a deep interest in the welfare of the governed, repressing lawlessness among the soldiery, and spending his fortune lavishly in order to avoid levies on the Piedmontese (*Mém.* III. 455–6). Finally, worn out by struggles and anxieties, so much so that he could use only his brain and his tongue (IV. 86), he hastened to France in the vain hope that he might transmit personal.y to the king 'many things for his service'

Probably the truth behind so phenomenal a change in characterization as exists between *Gargantua* and the *Tiers Livre* is that Rabelais' views having changed he had found himself ever more and more in harmony with his master; that he, like the Governor of Piedmont and Pantagruel, had found a greater scope for his personal geniality and wide vision, even though he necessarily felt most sensitively the inevitable isolation from his fellows[1]; and that therefore this, his greatest character study, was a composite of observation of his master and tentative self-study, the one carefully checked by the other. Not the crude objectivism or the arrogant self-assertion of his earlier books, but the modern blending of objective and subjective can be detected in his later characterization.

which ('craignant de faire tort à ceux qui en lui s'estoient fiez') he did not care to send by others. This consideration for his dependants and for the poor, and his reasoned contempt for prognostications (*Mém.* II. 325–6), he shared, *along with so much that being intimate may have been lost,* with the mature Pantagruel. Cp. *Mémoires de Martin et Guillaume du Bellay* (ed. V. L. Bourrilly et F. Vindry, 1908); V. L. Bourrilly, *Guillaume du Bellay, Seigneur de Langey*; and *R. S. S.* 1914, pp. 285–8.

[1] However closely Rabelais and his patron were related, the master would remain aloof from Rabelais' immediate circle, just as Pantagruel does. Possibly Rabelais' uncertainty in regard to introspective knowledge would explain some of Pantagruel's vagueness.

4. THE SOCIAL QUESTIONS

THERE are few interests in which we might more expect Rabelais' views to have been transformed by his passage from seclusion to public life, from privacy to the companionship of a notable statesman, than in his social teaching. And it may be said that there are few in which he is seen to have developed differently from his contemporaries. It has been said that he carefully followed the political movements of his time, and, except in the possible sense that he trimmed his sails to the favourable gale, this is undeniably true. The supposition that Rabelais was a time-server seems on a wide view of his works to be the most false of all traditional condemnations. Francis I's absolute rule preluded an astonishing growth of the nobility's power on the one hand and, at a later date, naturally of opposition from the bourgeois on the other, and we might expect that self-interest would incline Rabelais to the aristocratic, the more promising side. That it did not, that he appealed to the bourgeois, that, indeed, he may have assisted in the formation of the 'Politiques' party, there is abundant evidence; but that evidence must be sought in his work after 1546. From whatever angle we study *Pantagruel* and *Gargantua* we cannot fail to notice the unquestioning sympathy with aristocratic ideals and the arrogant disregard of lesser interests, which must have marked the man's character. Grandgousier, it is true, laments over his subjects, his 'flock,' whose property Picrochole was ravaging (G. 28), but that is certainly because Rabelais' social mentor, Plato, had likewise insisted that rulers existed for the good of their subjects. It is impossible to rely upon a slightly inconsistent utterance in the early books, and Rabelais, no less than his fellow-students, was inspired by the aristo-cratic Renaissance spirit.

Therefore, like any conventional knight, Pantagruel waged war, with Epistemon and Panurge as squires in attendance upon him (P. pp. 92–7), and the question of moral justification for war did not arise, because 'war is the only study of a prince.' Later, however, this question did arise in a very acute form. It was when the author of *Gargantua* had hit upon the idea of figuring under the thin covering of the war with Picrochole a family lawsuit[1], and when this 'war' affected a bourgeois king's prosperity. War then became evil in its effects, but, although the feeble monarch protested against his lawless neighbour's attacking him instead of resorting to arbitration, yet he proceeded without delay, and in the most approved aristocratic fashion, to the disposal of his enemy's property (G. 50). What matters the assurance that Picrochole's old subjects will receive better treatment than ever before? The story lacks conviction. Rabelais toyed with schemes for the humane settle-ment of conquered territory, but he never doubted

[1] W. F. Smith, *Rabelais in his Writings*, pp. 44 ff.

that the peoples should be taken over and should be at the absolute disposal of the conqueror. In this respect there is little change apparent between Pantagruel's settlement of Dipsodie (*P.* pp. 102 ff.) and Gargantua's: in both cases the new subjects welcome their new master with joy. Yet in the revision of his work he seems to have felt the need for some slight modification (*T. L.* 1), and so the conqueror selected his best subjects, those who were one with him in blood and customs, for settlement among the conquered. If the improvement is but small, it is still a guarantee that the new government shall conform to the standard of Utopia; and yet Panurge's governorship of Salmigondin would afford ample proof that Rabelais' humanity sat strange on him, that still his old notions of men wholly governed for the profit of their rulers dominated his mind[1]. With the development of his higher powers, however, there came a new attitude to the problem of war; and not even profound disapproval of wealth destroyed and injustices committed by the aggressors adequately represents his feeling. All wars, except those of defence, he wholeheartedly denounced because all their effects are evil and because their avowed cause is usually ignorance, and so wholly within man's control. But nothing short of a perusal of the

[1] Pantagruel's remonstrance with Panurge is based on his wishing to make the new governor rich. *T. L.* 1–8 is probably work of an earlier date than 1546.

Papefiguière episode, and still more of the fight with
the Andouilles, could fully convey the author's
sympathy with victims whom human ignorance or
treachery destroys. From mistaken notions—they
suspect invasion and unspeakable outrage—the terrified Andouilles rush to arms and ambush the
travellers, and even after the mistake has been
rectified we feel that Pantagruel's benevolent desire
to mediate between them and their oppressor will
prove vain. The principal difficulty, we know, will
not be the latter's refusal to be reconciled, but rather
the delusions under which the victims labour[1]. Given
the opportunity, the Andouilles would act in a similar
way to the Papimanes, whose suspicion, treachery and
fanaticism—all of which only enlightenment could
destroy—reduced Papefiguière to such a wretched
condition (*Q. L.* 45). This acute penetration to the
causes of war and this pity for perverse human nature
raise his treatment of the question on to an altogether
different plane. 'To avenge the insult to the Pope's
image, the Papimanes rushed to arms a few days
later without giving the slightest warning, surprised,
ravaged and ruined the whole island, and destroyed
with the edge of the sword every full-grown man';
and the travellers could not bear to penetrate far
into the country 'seeing the wretchedness and distress

---

[1] 'Plustost auriez vous les chats et ratz, les chiens et lievres
ensemble reconcilié' (*Q. L.* 35). Their religious prejudices had
become second nature.

of the people.' Of all Rabelais' unfortunates the poor
Papefigues lay nearest to his heart, and yet, since the
country apparently was rank with the grossest superstition, we may not so well account for it by supposed
Protestant sympathy as by his humane and enlightened
aspirations. The Prologue of the *Tiers Livre* had
breathed enthusiastic resistance to a foreign foe;
but resistance may be impossible, and Rabelais, the
patriot, perforce disappeared behind the man whose
enemy was ignorant prejudice.

On war and similar questions of high policy his
later utterances are few; and the reason is not far
to seek. He may have realized in the course of his
service with the Du Bellays that such matters
demanded special training which could not be his
lot. More probably he took a dislike for his old
musings because life proved them so vain. But, after
all, compared with the manifold petty injustices of
human life, compared with the excesses which he
saw everywhere[1] whose cumulative effect was none
the less real or harmful for their being elusive, wars
were rare. He set himself to track down these more
insidious evils. From the schemes of government,
monastery reform and education, with which he had
charmed his readers, his later books are free, and in
their place correction of human failings abounds. In

[1] Rabelais was aware of Aristotle's *Ethics* (G. 10), yet until
his later work he was apparently not concerned with human
behaviour. His advocacy of moderation in all things demonstrates a new outlook.

place of the chapters, which are necessarily marked
by that kind of detachment that may best be described
as aristocratic, we find the closest association of the
author with his fellows. The section on education,
for example, with its three distinct schemes[1], culminates in the education of the prince. The princely
pupil almost neglects the liberal arts, eloquence and
courtesy, to which Eudemon, the page, devoted so
much time and by which his education was judged,
and he spent long hours each day in physical exercises
that should fit him for his duties as a warrior. ('Car
telles choses servent a discipline militaire.') A perfect
seat in the saddle, perfect familiarity with swimming,
and extraordinary powers of endurance, along with
'how to break an enemy's lance' and the manipula-
tion of all the weapons in the armoury, were the
ideals of Gargantua's tutor. 'Il fust passé chevalier
d'armes en campagne' (G. 23). It is more purely
aristocratic than Pantagruel's education since the
earlier scheme did at any rate aim at making the
pupil 'an abyss of learning,' and did not include
instruction in chivalry. *That* the prince was to learn
after his 'education' had been completed ('il te
fauldra yssir de ceste tranquillite et repos destude,
et apprendre la cheualerie et les armes pour deffendre
ma maison, et noz amys secourir en tous leurs affaires
contre les assaulx des malfaisans,' *P.* p. 27). If the

---

[1] Holofernes' system is superseded by Ponocrates' education
of Eudemon and apparently that by his education of Gargantua.

THE SOCIAL QUESTIONS 75

Gargantuan system was an improvement upon that of Pantagruel, it must be in that it reduced the amount of learning to be acquired (and this is doubtful), and incorporated physical training[1]. The intellectual culture of Gargantua was, it is true, linked up with nature, but the study was apparently not destined for use, and much of it did not exceed the idlest of curiosity[2]. Thus on wet days they visited the shops of druggists, apothecaries and herbalists, they observed mountebanks' deceits, and they frequented law-courts, all of them admirable occupations no doubt were they destined to help the future monarch, but to judge by the phrasing certainly rather undertaken as a kind of amusement[3]. Pantagruel, as far as is known, did not follow such a course of training, and so we need not be surprised that when

[1] Rabelais appears thus to have made a long step towards reality. Eudemon, who spoke so well that he resembled a Gracchus, or a Cicero, or an Emilius of the past rather than a youth of that age (G. 15), was apparently less the author's ideal type of educated man than the practical warrior. In other places Rabelais allowed *sneers* at students to creep in, cp. G. 39: 'O le bon compaignon que cest! Mais quelle mousche la picqué? Il ne faict rien qu'estudier depuis je ne scay quand. Je nestudie poinct de ma part.'

[2] Though a version of humanist ideals, notably of Vittorino da Feltré's scheme (see Tilley, *François Rabelais*, p. 139), this is hardly noble disinterestedness.

[3] 'Alloit voir les basteleurs, trejectaires et theriacleurs, et consideroit leurs gestes, leurs ruses, leurs sobressaults et beau parler: singulierement de ceux de Chaunys en Picardie, car ilz sont de nature grands jaseurs et beaux bailleurs de baillivernes en matiere de cinges verds' (G. 24). In G. 45 Grandgousier said of priests: 'telz imposteurs empoisonnent les asmes.'

an admiring public offered him an honourable office
he refused it graciously because 'there was too much
work in such duties and those who carry them out
can hardly be saved from the common corruption of
mankind' (*P.* p. 44). With this we may conclude
that the author lacked interest in real matters. To
that may be attributed his amusement at the abuse of
the law, for the Humevesne episode and Pantagruel's
judgment on the case, and Janotus de Bragmardo's
'immortal' lawsuit (*G.* 20), could hardly be more
distantly removed from the Bridoye satire and the
Grippeminauld indignation. Yet we cannot believe
that legal corruption, which became more and more
pronounced later on[1], was at that time non-existent,
and we must infer that before his important change
of views Rabelais did not appreciate its effects or the
necessity for repressing it. But by far the most important proof of his aloofness from the ordinary
affairs of men may be found in the Abbey of Thelema.

The account of that airy structure is more remarkable for the evidence of architectural interests than
for its contribution to thought. It has, however, been
accepted as the expression of Rabelais' aspirations to
natural freedom and, rather differently, as a sketch
of a social Utopia; and both these views are attractive.
Yet it is somewhat difficult to believe that a state

---

[1] Cp. *R.S.S.* 1913 ('La Procédure en France'); and Villeroy's
Mémoires, pp. 27–9 (1636 ed.). 'Grippeminaux' were, of
course, excluded from Thelema.

of life, which relieved the inmates from contact with the greater part of humanity, can be regarded otherwise than as the comprehensive satire of all with whom the author disagreed, which we have noted on a former page[1]. Rabelais hated the monastic rules; he reduced the rules to one. Yet the inmates of the abbey did not apparently observe that one[2]. In short, as far as the thought in Thelema is concerned it would be easy to adduce irreconcilable elements in plenty. What is more important is that so common was the idea of reform of monasteries that Polydore Vergil[3] himself suggested complete liberty to leave the institution, as Rabelais himself did. Moreover about 1480 a real reform had been carried out through numerous students of noble birth entering monasteries as asylums in the then disturbed state of society. Is it not therefore probable that Rabelais had heard of this reform[4], and took advantage of it to plan an abbey which should be the 'opposite of all the others'? Instead of those who, according to Editus, flocked to the Isle Sonante[5], Rabelais proposed to allow noble

[1] P. 46.
[2] 'Fais ce que vouldras' is hardly compatible with the sympathy existing between men and women (G. 56) and its effects.
[3] De Inventoribus Rerum, Bk VII, c. 1.
[4] 'Cy entrez, vous, et bien soyez venus
    Et parvenus, tous nobles chevaliers' (G. 54).
[5] I. S. p. 11. Starving idlers, disappointed lovers, desperate men and criminals, as well as children who, remaining at home, would necessitate the dismemberment of estates.

men and women to enter and leave of their own free will. Long lists of those who must be excluded are given,—mainly the professions which he had generally and sweepingly ridiculed,—and of those who may be admitted (*G.* 54). Noble knights and ladies of high degree will, it appears, be able to live a communal life with 'gentle companions' and the reforming party. Within the walls business troubles neither man nor woman, and they amuse themselves as 'liberal-minded and well-educated people of good birth' ('gens liberes, bien nés, bien instruicts') may do. Even the question of marriage was postponed to the time when a man's worldly affairs forced him to leave the institution. 'Oh happy folks, oh demi-gods, would to Heaven that my life had been thus!' cried the author when Editus described the felicities of life in the Isle Sonante (*I. S.* p. 15), and that seems to have been his later attitude towards the ideal life of Thelema. The pictures purchased in Medamothi (*Q. L.* 2) may be seen 'in Thelema, on the left hand as you enter the main gallery,' and you may also see the Thelemites practising the art of Messer Gaster whereby cannon balls are stopped in mid-air and thrown back upon the enemy (*Q. L.* 62). Rabelais would seem to have formed a contemptuous estimate of one of his pleasantest compositions and he then turned it into a kind of Pays de Satin, a land of impossibilities. Like Homenas and Editus, he had dreamed of passing his life free from worries and cares, aloof from the majority of his fellows, maintained in mysterious fashion and certainly serving no clearly defined social purpose. For surely Rabelais and all other reformist-students ('gentilz compaignons'), along with knights and ladies, could enter Thelema leaving the unpleasant world behind them. Unlike Homenas and Editus, he had renounced his cloistered life, he had chosen the everyday world; and his cold selfish ambitions had left no trace behind them. So the memory of those ideals provoked his amusement.

It was inevitable that all non-lettered and humble interests should suffer in the first two books. The author of *Thelema* seems hardly to have been aware of their existence; and when he desires to punish the unjust Picrochole he refers to his calling 'as a poor labourer in Lyons, as choleric as ever' (*G.* 49). Why this detachment? Perhaps the truth is that he was in his polemical stage, in consequence of which he looked on everything that did not affect his active interests with a grossly ignorant indifference. Thus, in spite of his recognition of learned women ('Il nest pas les femmes et filles qui ne ayent aspire a ceste louange et a ceste manne celeste de bonne doctrine,' *P.* p. 26), woman generally received such treatment as has been accepted in proof of his constant and considered hostility to her. Yet it cannot well be disputed that the later work betrays an ever-increasing respect both for woman and for parenthood[1]; and

[1] Cp. *Q. L.* 9 and *I. S.* p. 11.

this remarkable development surely implies that
Rabelais came to know true womanly worth better.
It may imply much more than this. The portraiture
of the 'haulte dame de Paris[1]' is astonishingly exact
and convincing. She appears to have been a very
worthy, self-respecting and modest *bourgeoise* whose
chief misfortune was that a worthless vagrant had
set his heart on winning her, and the interest of
the readable part of the story as told is wholly in the
ingenuity with which Panurge attempted to convert
strong resistance into compliance. If, however, as is
our modern way, we read the story with sympathy
for the lady, we shall see that we have contributed
what Rabelais lacked, and that the point of the story
is fundamentally changed[2]. Rabelais had probably no
pity for the lady, nor had he any for Gargamelle who
died for joy at her son's home-coming[3], but he could
have chosen stories much more damaging to the lady's
character from the storehouse of medieval literature.
Certainly the whole point of the story would be lost,

[1] Surely there is a sneer in this description of a citizen's wife,
or is it that to the poor student the lady's rank seemed more
exalted than it was?

[2] Thus the phrase most (superficially) damaging to the lady's
character ('Mais elle cemmenca a sescryer toutefois non pas trop
hault') is explained, but *naturally not by the author*, by her fear
that her husband should discover and misinterpret Panurge's
possession of her rosary—which Panurge had torn from her in
church.

[3] 'Car *Supplementum Supplementi Chronicorum* dit que Gargamelle y mourut de joie: je n'en sçay rien de ma part, *et bien
peu me soucie ny d'elle ny d'aultre*' (G. 37).

were there not—as at the present day there is not—
a tacitly agreed contempt for unexpected if homely
virtue between the author and his readers. The
author of *Pantagruel* could therefore find pleasure
in traditional jests at the expense of woman, and
yet, although in treating the question of Panurge's
marrying he appears not entirely to have cast off the
fetters of the past, he would needs later have to place
Panurge's former victim among those worthy women
for whom Rondibilis had undisguised and unbounded
admiration. 'Seulement vous diray que petite nest la
louange des preudes femmes, lesquelles ont vescu
pudiquement et sans blasme, et ont en la vertu de
ranger cestuy effrene animal a l'obeissance de la
raison' (*T. L.* 32). No doubt the consideration that
his indebtedness to Tiraqueau's book might reconcile
the two estranged friends[1] had weight with the
author of the *Tiers Livre*; but neither that nor the
new purpose in thus consecrating so much space,
certainly not a whole book, to the discussion of
marriage need turn us from the main point. Below
the superficial unpleasantness we cannot help seeing
that Rabelais is considering a practical problem that
may affect the humble as well as the great; that he
is weighing evidence; and that without good reason
he no longer ridicules views with which he cannot
sympathize. It is likewise remarkable that Pantagruel,
who opposed many of the researches, should propose

[1] *R. E. R.* vol. IV, pp. 384–9.

and justify consultations with a theologian, a doctor, and a lawyer on the ground that they must be reliable whose social responsibilities are so great. And these practical men, Pantagruel, Rondibilis, Hippothadée (and even Trouillogan), giving substantially the same advice, it is remarkable that the physician Rondibilis is on the whole very favourable to woman.

Concerned primarily with the place marriage occupies in nature, Rondibilis opened his speech with words comprehensible to the lowest intelligence of that day, and alleged the customary charges against woman. She is variable, uncertain and imperfect. Nature seems to have made a mistake when she created woman, and the only conclusion to come to is that woman ought to provide the social delights of man rather than seek any perfection of her 'individual femininity' (*T. L.* 32). He then goes on to consider the main problem in marriage, the control of that 'animal' (for according to Aristotle's definition we should so style it) by which woman's 'whole body is shaken, all her sense ravished away, all her affections interrupted and her thoughts thrown into confusion'; and this control is possible. It is certain that many women have learned to curb the animal's power; and finally,—to omit much discussion which mainly proves that Rabelais had forestalled objections from his contemporaries,—Rondibilis adduces a new argument in the fable of the god Coquage (*T. L.* 33). He therein hints that by restricting woman's natural

freedom man himself had caused marital infidelity;
that unless the husband offers up sacrifices of suspicion,
mistaking, spying and enquiry to the god he will be
abandoned by the god and 'left to rot without a rival,
alone with his wife.' In spite therefore of the following
chapter of hilarity[1] we may affirm that Rabelais had
nearly approached the conclusion that marriage must
be founded on mutual trust and mutual help. In this
fable alone he had made amends for previous slanders
of woman, and we need hardly add that the theologian's
and Pantagruel's opinions, both to the same effect
though starting from *different* reasonings, weightily
confirm our view that Rabelais' attitude to the question was vastly improved[2]. The charming pictures of
Queen Niphleseth (*Q. L.* 42) and of the equally
attractive lady of Entelechie (*Quint Livre*, 20–3) are
slighter than that of the 'haulte dame,' but they are
neither more accurately observed nor more delicately
portrayed. Not the character of woman but the
artist's vision was changed; and his sympathetic power
enlarged. For Panurge and his kind there might still

[1] A notable instance of what has been seen to be one of
Rabelais' humorous effects, see pp. 34–5. It would seem that
Rondibilis' argument had reached its conclusion.
[2] The theologian says that Panurge's marriage will be happy
if he chooses a wife from a virtuous family, accustomed to
virtuous life. It is perhaps in Hippothadée's conclusion that we
must find Rabelais' main agreement with him: 'Ainsi serez vous
a vostre femme en patron et exemplaire de vertuz et honnesteté'
(*T. L.* 30). Pantagruel's opinion is even closer to that of Rondibilis, cp. *T. L.* 35.

be a problem in marriage, but for Pantagruel and for
Rabelais there could be none. The simplest phrase
utters the sincerest conviction. When Gargantua
urges his son to marry, the prince says he is quite
prepared to do so whensoever his father wishes and
to the lady whom he will choose (*T. L. 48*).

Whence then had these revaluations sprung?
Possibly as a result of his own marriage[1], but more
probably that had itself come about as a result of
his old haughty studentlike individualism suffering
eclipse. His struggles with the real world had effected
in him a wholesome change, and more definite social
notions had evolved. In like manner the doctrinaire
creation of Utopian schemes of government was
abandoned and forgotten. *Gargantua* owes much to
the attempted embodiment of Platonist principles,
and Grandgousier's statecraft was founded upon the
theory that a ruler-philosopher must ensure good
government. Yet when Panurge, having actually
failed as governor of Salmigondin, sketched an ideal
state of Debtors and Borrowers, in full conformity
with a universe of which one part borrows from an
ever-ready lending part, his friendly patron resisted
the argument and refuted it. The passage cannot be

---

[1] Being in orders Rabelais could not, of course, be legally
married. Boyssonné's poems on Rabelais' son, who 'when he
lived had Roman prelates for his attendants,' would seem to
indicate a truly fatherly pride in his little son, and therefore
a marital relation which in earlier years would have been
impossible.

other than a satire on his previous notions[1]. The
reader beholds the downfall of a prosperous province
under Panurge's reckless hands, and he must feel
sceptical of that ingenious transcendentalist's powers,
however satisfied he may be—under the spell of
Panurge's facile eloquence—to silence his doubts.
At last, however, the whole dreamy structure is
levelled with the ground by Pantagruel's simple citation of Plato's *Laws*. It was the first attempt of many
which show clearly the author's mistrust of such
academic systems. Into the mouth of Homenas, of
Editus, of Hippothadée—all representatives of what
Rabelais could not accept—he put schemes which
should infallibly restore the golden age; and the whole
Isle d'Ennasin can bear but one interpretation. The
author could no longer avoid laughing at states
fashioned according to an intellectual conception,
transcendental or otherwise; he could not view the
negation of human relationships in the interests of
a state. In a certain definite sense his preoccupation
with the abuses of his day postulates and confirms
this as his natural way of thinking. Ideal states are
radically destructive while reform implies some
measure of conservatism; and the doctrinaire philosopher inclines to disregard the happiness of individuals, while with Rabelais the happiness of simple

[1] Millet (*François Rabelais*, in 'Les Grands Ecrivains Français,' pp. 65–6) interprets Panurge's scheme as proof that
Rabelais held lofty views on social relations. In Turin Rabelais
had seen a province almost destroyed by Panurge's methods.

people became more and more important[1]. Thus
while the old Grandgousier had protested against the
poisoning of his subjects' souls (G. 45), the new
Gargantua bitterly attacked the 'pastophores taulpetiers[2],' and Pantagruel the Engastrimythes (Q. L.
58), because they destroyed the happiness and deceived
the hopes of common folk,—a preoccupation with
the welfare of the governed which might still be in
tune with a principle of Platonism, but of a Platonism
of which more than half had been rejected. And along
with this concern for the real welfare of the people
occur some incidental references, of a denunciatory
kind, to other classes in society. The 'small devil,'
behaving with all the arrogance of the first Pantagruel,
receives as little sympathy as the foolish 'janspill'-
hommes' whose avarice leads to their downfall[3].

[1] Cp. Prologue, Q. L. Couillatris' axe must be restored to
him: it is as important to him as a kingdom to its king; and
Q. L. 44, where it is seen that, however cheaply the Ruach
islanders may live, even then they have their cares.
[2] T. L. 48: 'Et voyent les dolens peres et meres hors leurs
maisons enlever, et tirer par un incongneu, estrangier, barbare
...leurs tant belles, delicates, riches et saines filles, lesquelles
tant cherement avoient nourries....Et restent en leurs maisons,
prives de leurs filles tant aimees le pere mauldissant le jour et
heure de ses nopces; la mere regrettant que nestoit avortee en tel
triste et malheureux enfantement; et en pleurs et lamentations
finent leur vie.'
[3] In the early books there is contempt of wealth and of the
avaricious, but no indignation, cp. the usurers in Hell (P.
p. 101): 'Je les veiz tous occupez a chercher les espingles rouil-
lees, et vieulx cloux, parmy les ruisseaulx des rues, comme
vous voyez que font les coquins en ce monde!'

Merchants, men of law, doctors and judges fall under the same condemnation as the noble and the gentlemen; and the poor peasants themselves—the Jacques Bonhommes—are no less given to the vice of desiring enormous wealth by any and every means (Prol. *Q. L.*). The marriage institution itself is likewise corrupted by mercenary considerations. It is not merely that the common people are bound to suffer under such conditions, but rather that the vicious do themselves a real injury. That seems to be the thought at the back of his mature denunciations, and it is easily seen how the old disinterested student could have thus developed.

Rabelais' mature opinion seems then to have been that we must accept the State as by law established[1], but that we may and must submit each and every member of it to our closest scrutiny with a view to amending their ways. Everywhere and in every rank he had detected this vice of personal greed, and to such an extent did he inveigh against it that we might be misled into supposing that the old student's disinterestedness had warped his judgment[2], were it not

---

[1] Cp. *A. P.* where he protests that nothing in his books is intended to offend God, the king, or any other. He would, however, have laws made amending the powers and privileges of the pastophores (*T. L.* 48), cp. *I. S.* pp. 20–1.

[2] In *Q. L.* 25 Pantagruel assured the old Macrobe that they had escaped the Storm because they did not seek gain as merchants, but were impelled by a desire to learn. Such utterances are, however, rare in the later section.

for confirmation from other sources[1], and if he did
not single out other faults. Lawyers, he hints, were
not concerned with justice. The fact was notorious
that they adopt causes that they know to be unjust;
and in his fellows' opinion Judge Bridoye was proved
guilty chiefly of shortening interminable lawsuits by
resort to the dice box[2]. It was his transgression against
the professional code, and not, as in the case of the
Chats Fourrés, that he did not do his best to dispense
judgments, that brought him, old and infirm, before Trinquamelle. The Chats Fourrés, however,
were guilty of the most incredible ambitions. They
travestied the law because primarily they sought universal dominion, just as the somewhat ridiculous
Chiquanous sought local power[3]. Government officials
and tax-collectors were likewise to be denounced,
but the passage is so obviously incomplete that only
oppression may be laid to their account (*I. S.* pp. 36–
41). Men of science were also ridiculed on account
of the utter uselessness or the impossibility of their

[1] Lavisse (*Histoire*, etc. vol. v, pp. 243–75) traces it to the
relaxation of Church laws against usury. Cp. Villeroy's
Mémoires, vol. I, p. 23 (1636 ed.), and D'Aubigné, *Sa Vie à ses
Enfants* in the well-known scene where Henry IV taunts his
followers with avarice.

[2] Cp. Bragmardo's *immortal* lawsuit for Rabelais' earlier
treatment (*G.* 20).

[3] In *Q. L.* 12, where the Chiquanous deprive a gentleman of
his estate and sometimes cast him into prison to rot in misery;
in *T. L.* 44 Epistemon denounces faulty judges; in Prol. *Q. L.*
Jupiter's dog would, like the advocates and Dandin, allow no
animal to escape it.

researches (*Quint Livre*, 22); and several times he sneered at the false prescriptions of men of his own profession. Thus he quotes against them or allows Bridoye to quote the common proverb, 'Heureux est le medecin qui est appelle sus la declination de la maladie' (*T. L.* 41). There is no firm doctrine herein, but these utterances do at least point to a social ideal of which he was vaguely conscious, and by which it was possible to help mankind.

Of this ideal we catch glimpses from time to time. Wealth, for instance, must perform a necessary function in society, and even if it be used in the pursuit of truth and learning that would perhaps be a legitimate purpose[1]. But those who neglect their social duties in order to acquire it, and those who possessing it undervalue and squander it, are certainly considered to be in the highest degree blameworthy. There can be little doubt that Rabelais blamed the foolish, spendthrift governor of Salmigondin, and the gamblers of the Isle of Cassade (*I. S.* p. 23), equally with the petty malversations of Homenas, though less

[1] In appointing Panurge governor of Salmigondin Pantagruel seems to have had the idea of making him rich (*T. L.* 2), although the author had just written of him: 'Car tous les biens que le ciel couvre, et que la terre contient en toutes ses dimensions...ne sont dignes desmouvoir noz affections et troubler nos sens et esprits.' In spite of its resemblance to *G.* 33 ('Thesaurizer est faict de vilain'), it is in Panurge's reply that the earlier attitude is rather to be traced: 'Riche? respondit Panurge. Aviez vous là fermé vostre pensée?...Tout le monde crie mesnaige, mesnaige; mais tel parle de mesnaige, qui ne scait mie que c'est.' Certainly Panurge did not, while Pantagruel protested against ridiculous extravagance.

than the enormities of Grippeminauld. And the real
difference between these various instances is that the
latter two affect in varying degrees the welfare of
others while gamblers and spendthrifts merely harm
themselves. Social well-being, he considered, depends
principally upon the moral character of the men and
women who compose society, and consequently he
applied himself to the task of amending by satire or
by fierce denunciations the faults that he had noted.
His old dreams of 'doing what he wished' must have
given way before considerations which had prompted
him to enquire how far individual freedom may be
permitted and how far the claims of society must,
through custom, be allowed to restrain the individual
(*T. L.* 7). To be sure he had no solution to offer on
that subject, but it is obvious that his thoughts must
have travelled far from their point of departure. It
appears almost inevitable that so profound a change
should have come about through his life in one of
the political circles of his time. The shifting demands
of worldly activity would naturally throw into confusion a mind that had loved to frequent the realm
of abstractions and that had been guided by the light
of the Absolute; and it was from *his* visit to *his*
oracle, the facts of existence, that Rabelais had brought
back truths which he had discovered, and which,
having their roots firmly in human nature, appear
so astounding when seen in contrast with what a more
refined age necessarily considered coarse.

5. THE AUTHORITY OF ANCIENT LITERATURE[1]

So much Renaissance work was vitiated by blind obedience to classical authority, to the written word, that it has been said that that great movement gave birth to nothing. At the least this is surprising. The great Greeks had shown themselves supremely independent in thought, independent of the conventional views of their day, and capable of most virile criticism; and we should expect the students to reproduce a similar intellectual freedom. Generally speaking they did not; and, though it seems beyond doubt that only in that time of upheaval we may hope to discover demarcation lines between what was medieval and what modern, we search in vain among the greater number of the literary works for signs of modernity. Such signs must however exist. The workers for modern views in the seventeenth century, whose work appears on a superficial survey to have come upon the world with bewildering suddenness, must have had precursors in the preceding age. In all probability ideas spring from actual tentatives, and the freedom of the poets of 1660, and their devotion to common sense in literary theory, cannot possibly have developed out of the rule-bound later sixteenth century school: indeed, in La Bruyère's opinion, we must retrace our steps much further. All kinds

[1] This section appeared under the heading 'Rabelais and the Authority of the Ancients' in *The Modern Language Review* of January, 1923.

of authority tend to support the one the other. Civil
authority upholds the Church; Church authority upholds the accepted traditional ways of thought; and
the teaching of the day in so far as it is authoritative
tends to support both Church and State. It is therefore at a time when not only orthodoxy was challenged
by reform, but also when the basis of society came
under discussion, that the dead hand of classical
literature would also be thrown off, rather than when
the counter-reform movement had somewhat re-
established orthodox power. A very sure instinct had
caused the powerful in France to set their faces
against the New Learning, against the enthusiasm
for new visions which seems to have driven Rabelais
to grasp at every observable fact. In consequence,
just as the scholastics had at last distorted classical
teaching and by subordinating it to Church teaching
and patristic literature[1] had reconciled irreconcilable
philosophies, so wherever, during this period in
France, we can trace reverence for authority or for
the letter of authority, we may also find such an
amalgamation of pagan and Christian ideas as resulted,
to their mutual loss, in making both almost unrecog-
nizable[2]. Marguerite of Angoulême was at the head

[1] Thus Lefèvre d'Etaples curiously blended Platonism and
Aristotelianism, while lesser men, like Polydore Vergil, composed most naïvely learned treatises.
[2] Cp. Homenas' account of the coming of the decretals
from Heaven (Q. L. 49); and see Calvin's denunciation of the
third section, the literary men, p. 7, n. 1.

of Neo-Platonists whose aims were to reconcile Christian doctrine with Plato's metaphysics; and a long time was still to pass before Aristotelians definitely separated from the Catholic Church.

Intellectual and other eccentricities must of necessity exist in such an age. They are possibly the surest of warrants that the germs of race-development were active. They should be considered as vital attempts to adjust human affairs to a widened and widening vision; and it is hard to select an epoch of more varied extravagances than that of Rabelais. To what extent can it be proved that Rabelais floated with the current? How far did his powerful nature assert itself? The question is not whether he made use of his classical studies; that he did so is in the nature of things. Rather we must ask, and we may with confidence hope to discover what use he actually did make of his reading. We must seek to know whether he too meekly followed in the accustomed tracks. That is the all-important point; and when we consider for a moment that, in contrast with the neglect into which his contemporaries' writings have fallen, Rabelais' work has made a wide appeal to men of every age, we cannot hesitate to infer that *Pantagruel* as a whole possesses distinctive characteristics that have sustained, and may have increased, its value.

In regard to his reverence for the ancients, the Rabelais of *Pantagruel* and of *Gargantua* was no more advanced than his age; and one result has been that from those books reforming zeal and the various classical enthusiasms have been carefully extracted, and over-emphasized in order to demonstrate the most curious ideals in the developed artist. The two books are a confusion. For his own purposes Rabelais must needs have blended most incongruous and incompatible notions, grossness and transcendentalism and Christian teaching. He could not well do otherwise. Through his ignorance of most of human concerns he was, at that time, in spite of one amusing reference to Pliny[1], demonstrably uncritical. Indeed, even in this attack on Pliny's veracity there appears a broad tolerance of an admired authority to whom in one instance he could feel agreeably superior; and this learned vanity found ample scope in his over-fond use of references and in his quotations from curious writers on obscure subjects[2]. Illustrations are found on every page in connection with the most commonplace statements. He makes no statement without some such confirmation. Quite unnecessarily, as it may seem, he quotes Orus Apollo and Polyphilus on the colours of Gargantua's dress:

[1] 'Et toutefois je ne suis poinct menteur tant asceure comme il a este' (*G.* 6).

[2] *P.* pp. 78–9: Panurge tests the lady's letter to Pantagruel for secret writing; *P.* p. 63: Thaumaste consults Pantagruel on magic, geomancy and the Caballa (though the passage implies ridicule, it is rather of Thaumaste than of the subjects). In *Gargantua* we note the virtues of precious stones, significance of colours, etc.

Bien aultrement faisoient en temps jadis les saiges d'Egypte,
quand ilz escrivoient par lettres quilz appelloient hiero-
glyphiques...lesquels un chascun entendoit qui entendist
la vertu, propriete et nature des choses par icelles figurees.
Desquelles Orus Apollon a en grec compose deux livres,
et Polyphile, au Songe d'Amours, en a davantaige expose
(G. 9).

The author's mind leaped easily from the colours to
hieroglyphic writing, and then reference became his
natural device. With much greater appropriateness he
adorned the account of Saint Aignan's bell (P. p. 21):

which was in the ground for nearly three hundred years
for it was so big that by no mechanism could they raise
it even out of the earth, although they applied all the means
that Vitruvius on architecture, Albertus on building,
Euclid, Theon, Archimedes and Hero on machines
suggest, for it was all of no avail.

That his references shall be so suitable can never,
however, be depended upon. In justification of
Pantagruel's seizing the affected Limousin student
by the throat, he quoted Aulus Gellius and Julius
Caesar who defend purity of language[1]; and when
he described the great drought and the great drops
of water that rose from the earth he naturally followed it up with a quotation from Seneca on the

---

[1] P. p. 21: 'Et apres quelques annees mourut de la mort de
Roland, ce faisant la vengeance divine, et nous demonstrant ce
que dit le Philosophe et Aulus Gellius, quil nous convient parler
selon le langaige usite. Et comme disoit Cesar, quil fault eviter
les motz absurdes en pareille diligence que les patrons de
navires evitent les rochiers de la mer.'

source of the Nile[1]. It would appear reasonable to conclude that he could not avoid this display of learning; indeed rather his reading probably dominated a mind that sincerely revered the ancient authors. And, as we have seen, the *Gargantua* is marked by the same characteristic. Rabelais had doubtless not begun to speculate on realities, or his speculations were at most embroidered with meretricious ornaments. In so far as his works bear evidence, he was in little superior to the author of *De Inventoribus Rerum*.

In *Gargantua*, however, much that was so inappropriate was certainly avoided, but this was only at the cost of swearing absolute fidelity to Platonism which contributed to purify and idealize his conceptions; and he appears to have set out with the notion of advocating his master's philosophy in all questions of the day, if we may judge by the Prologue[2]. The government of Picrochole, or Injustice, begets among his followers Discord and Strife. They contend, like Thrasymachus in the *Republic*, that the justice of the State should serve the interests of the

---

[1] *P.* p. 10: 'Les aultres gens scavans disoient que cestoit pluye des Antipodes: comme Senecque narre au quart livre questionum naturalium, parlant de lorigine et source du fleuve du Nil.'

[2] 'Car en icelle bien aultre goust trouverez et doctrine plus absconse, laquelle vous revelera de tres haults sacrements et mysteres horrifiques, tant en ce qui concerne nostre religion que aussi l'estat politiq et vie œconomique.' The whole Prologue breathes Platonism.

strong; and the contrast is great when we study the conditions of Grandgousier's subjects. That incarnation of Justice and Platonist King-philosopher is followed by Concord and Harmony; and he of course maintains that the true function of a King is to protect the weak and the inferior. Necessarily, therefore, when the war was almost over the 'punishment' of the captive Touquedillon was carried through on the most approved principles[2]. If we grant that his lord Picrochole had been unjust in making war on Grandgousier, he would have been made still more unjust by being truly punished, and consequently he received his liberty and gifts. It is, maybe, exceedingly difficult to conceive the state of mind which could regard that scene as anything but impracticable. To the minds of practical bourgeois Grandgousier's benevolence must have appeared as incredible as the Abbey of Thelema. And the same reason exists in both episodes. We have seen above that the idea behind Thelema was probably a reform of the monasteries. Into that was woven the Platonic relationship, based on the most perfect sympathy. Their manner of life even to questions of dress and amusements was consequently in perfect harmony. 'In this

[1] The idle concern with his story, or alternatively his excessive reverence for Platonism, is shown in the very earthly settlement of conquered kingdoms that follows. Transcendentalism had no message on such questions as yet, whereas later (*Q. L.* 42) humanity compelled Pantagruel to decline Niphleseth's submission.

freedom, they all entered into emulation to do what
they saw pleased one. If some man or woman said:
"Let us drink," they all drank. If they said: "Let
us play a game," they all played' (G. 57)—and so
forth. The lack of a sense of humour that should be
affected by such a scene could only be found in a
sincere and reverent pupil; and the book suggests in
every part that *Gargantua* was an intellectual and not
an emotional attempt. To return to the Abbey, the
sympathy resulted in effecting the marriage of any
man, who was forced by circumstances to leave the
Abbey, with the lady with whom he felt the closest
affinity; and 'just as they had lived well at Thelema
in devoted friendship, they continued to live still
better in marriage; and so they loved one another to
the end of their days, as well as they had done on the
first day of their married life.' If we did not reflect
that the Abbey bore the same relation to other abbeys
as Universal Justice and Love bear to human justice
and love, it would indeed be difficult to believe that,
with all this temporary quiet idealism, Rabelais really
conceived such harmony as resulting from the ideal
freedom of Thelema. The realist in Rabelais had not
detected the serious inconsequences of the account.
The realist in Rabelais had wholly surrendered to
Platonism in regard to statesmanship, and social life;
and it is quite possible that the characters, besides
being the incarnations of virtues and vices, may have
been drawn out on a Platonist basis. It may be that,

having created the grossly amusing Panurge, Rabelais added the admirably spirited Friar who lacked even his later coarseness for reasons explained above, and he may have planned to form out of them and a transformed Pantagruel embodiments of the Platonist trinity, the sensual, the spirited and the rational in human nature[1]. Certainly the plan, here suggested, was never carried through, but in Epistemon's later character signs are not lacking that such a notion may have been entertained. But this theory cannot and need not be pressed; in the other portions of *Gargantua* we have seen reason enough to conclude that between the publication of his first and second books, when the influence of Lyons society was strong upon him, Rabelais planned to attempt the diffusion of Platonism. Thence resulted the perplexing inconsistencies between the prince and his forbears. Thence also the blending of Platonist philosophy and Christian doctrine in Grandgousier's statecraft,—with a stronger admixture of the former than the latter. Finally the vast contrast between the two books was the outcome of this: indeed the only connecting link seems to be the reverence for Ancient Authority which, indiscriminate in *Pantagruel*, was specialized in *Gargantua*. Platonism, the real charm of the second part, made the wavering reformers like

---

[1] Panurge, Friar John and Pantagruel could then continue to act and speak in their old manner. Their progress would be an allegory of the individual's life.

Voulté enthusiastic admirers of Rabelais' genius, for his work was thus far in accordance with their own aims, and certainly it was the power that raised his invention to a nobler plane. Other forces were however working within him. He was not satisfied with a task which had brought fame within his reach. Heroet's version of the *Symposium*, *La Parfaicte Amye*, won the admiration of the sadly stricken Third Party in 1542, and though we know that Rabelais was then about to study Plato once more[1], he must have been also planning the *Tiers Livre* in which, amid profuse quotations from his one-time master, the ideas are decidedly hostile to all that Platonism represented. A surprising development at such a moment! We should have expected rather that he would rally to the side of the Queen of Navarre, the sole remaining hope of reformers and men of letters. Still more surprising is the fact that from 1546 onwards his quotations and references seem to be made with a view to quite new effects: most often he does not acknowledge his indebtedness; and when he does so, he becomes deplorably careless in regard to those authors whose views he could not share, attributing to one the doctrine of another. During the period of 1535 to 1546 he had probably stood aside from the humanist movement, and with a broader life had come a change of his attitude to Ancient Authority.

[1] See postscript of letter to Antoine Hullot.

The times were not ready for critical appreciation,
for discrimination between Platonism and what passed
current for it, and, it must be remembered, the
accuracy of Rabelais' scholarship has been seriously
impugned. Therefore that he seems to have dissociated
himself from the contemporary school of Neo-
Platonists[1], in the main feminist, is of importance.
Not only did he deliver shrewd blows in the weakest
part of their armour, but he also ridiculed many
of the currently accepted doctrines. He described
Panurge's women associates with whom he con-
sumed the revenues of Salmigondin as Platonists and
Ciceronians; he invoked Plato's authority for his
doubts whether woman be an animal or a reasoning
creature[2], although—as we have seen—Rondibilis
had a higher opinion of her; and there is an analogous
intention in the discussion of foretelling the future
by seeing one's genius[3]. Moreover there is a passage
possibly indicative of the common tendency to weld
Platonist and Christian elements into one whole:
le serpent qui tenta Eve estoit andouillicque: ce nonobstant
est de luy escrit qu'il estoit fin et cauteleux sus tous les

[1] His dedication to Margaret of Navarre of the *Tiers Livre*
does not invalidate this view. He recognizes therein that his
Pantagruel is of the earth, earthy, while the queen's mind is in
heaven.

[2] 'Certes Platon ne scait en quel rang il les doibve colloquer,
ou des animans raisonnables, ou des bestes brutes' (*T. L.* 32).

[3] 'Aucuns Platoniques (says Epistemon) disent que qui peut
voir son genius peut entendre ses destinées. Je ne comprends pas
bien leur discipline, et ne suis d'advis que y adherez. Il y a
de l'abus beaucoup' (*T. L.* 24).

aultres animans. Aussi sont Andouilles. Encores maintient-
on *en certaines academies* que ce tentateur estoit l'andouille
nommée Ityphalle, en laquelle fut jadis transformé le bon
messer Priapus (*Q. L.* 38).

From such passages we might possibly infer that
Rabelais had realized the need for purifying the Neo-
Platonism of the day at least of elements with which
he disagreed; and that in itself would mark a great
advance. We cannot however rest there because elsewhere, by a method of satire which he commonly
adopted (that of giving actual expression to an impossibility, of realizing the impossible), he appears to
have attacked a more fundamental principle.

With reference to the suggested examination of
dream divination, he wrote:

Now there is no need to prove it at greater length. You will
understand it by a common illustration. You know, when
children, well washed and well fed, are sleeping soundly,
the nurses go off amusing themselves in perfect freedom
as if for that time permitted to do what they wish, for their
presence about the cradle would seem to be useless. In
this way, when the body sleeps, the soul takes its pleasure
and visits its homeland, which is heaven (*T. L.* 13).

Thence it returns bearing memories of past, present
and future events, for in heaven nothing passes away,
and every future event is apparent, and so it appears
to be endowed with prophecy; and many authorities,
but specially the Greeks, confirm this belief[1]. At

[1] Heraclitus, Holy Scripture and profane history are quoted.
At the same time, he says, many people are known never to
have dreamed.

first it may appear doubtful whether we must not accept this argument as a serious exposition of Platonist metaphysics, but there are too many discordant hints mingled with the theory. All that is real and earthly contrasts sharply with the transcendental: the nurse's neglect of her duties, her amusements while her charge slept and the subtle parallel between her gossip (of past, present and future) and heaven, all suggest the older stories too clearly to be overlooked. Besides, Rabelais' subsequent adoption of conventional description[1],—a very unusual proceeding with him,—and his insistence that Panurge must 'put away all human feelings, love, hatred, hope and fear,' would seem to make a satirical intention certain. And in the upshot, in spite of the thoroughness of their discussion and the serious doctrines touched upon, Panurge refused to go to bed without supper and had to be earnestly persuaded even to modify his usual diet. He cannot sleep without a good meal and the authorities insist on their dreamers doing so, or being very moderate. At last he agreed to try, but even then suggested the use of laurel twigs placed under his pillow in accordance with tradition; to which Pantagruel answered: 'There is no need. That's merely a superstition and those writers who recommend it are abusing their readers.' It appears no less probable that the matter-of-fact Rabelais would

[1] 'Sus l'heure que la joyeuse Aurora aux doigts rozatz dechassera les tenebres nocturnes.'

soon or late have disputed with transcendentalism than that the laughter generated by Panurge's unwillingness to comply with all the conditions must have affected the philosophic views quoted in advance. To what end, the readers must have cried, all this quotation of classical writers if the results are to be so ridiculous?

In each quest, it must be recalled, the author's plan was the same. The suggestion of a further search was followed by a fairly extensive review of authorities and ultimately the test was sometimes made with all proper conditions observed, sometimes avoided. Finally, however, the problem was found to be solvable only by individual judgment. The *Tiers Livre* treated not only of marriage, not only of the futility of divination; it was a sustained satire of traditional and uncritical learning[1]. Indeed the whole book suggests that Rabelais principally desired to envelop the tyrannical Ancients' authority in absurdities which a new generation was coming to regard in their true light, and in traditional ways of thought which bourgeois common sense, that fount of 'libertinism,' was

---

[1] Cp. *T. L.* 52: 'Ne me paragonnez poinct icy la salamandre. Cest abus. Je confesse bien que petit feu de paille la vegete et resjouit. Mais je vous asceure qu'en grande fournaise elle est, comme tout aultre animant, suffoquee et consumee. Nous en avons veu l experience. Galen lavoit, longtemps a, conferme et demonstre.' This passage shows his dependence upon one author to dispute a common belief.

soon to discredit[1]. The usually exuberant Rabelais seems at least once to have wearied of his heavy task of selecting from the abundant material for this purpose. At least once he contemptuously refused to proceed. 'Yet Cicero, said Pantagruel, says something or other about it in his second book on Divination' ('Toutesfois, dist Pantagruel, Ciceron en dist je ne scay quoy au second livre de Divination'—*T. L.* 20). Material was too abundant, and his purpose too clear to his mind to admit of doubt. How then had he reached this conclusion? Two passages in the book may conceivably illustrate his development. When he had described Panurge's Utopia of Debtors and Borrowers and had attempted to make out a transcendental justification for it, his thoughts had wandered to the hostile thought of Plato's *Laws* (*T. L.* 3–5); and when he came to consider the consultation of the dumb he had been struck by the lack of unanimity among classical writers on the question (*T. L.* 19). It appears in the highest degree probable that the earlier enthusiast for Plato's transcendentalism had received a shock on reading Plato's *Laws*, that his experience and wider conversation and reading had sobered him, and that in the labour of accumulating material for his work on divinatory methods or on the marriage question he had learned to weigh the evidence and to discriminate between the values of ancient authors.

[1] The author of the *Pantagrueline Prognostications* must already have stood for disbelief in divination.

What renders this demonstration difficult is his
decided preference for undermining rather than
directly attacking his enemy's positions[1]. Nevertheless the inference is clear when Jupiter, busy settling
human disputes, not merely has no leisure to decide
between Ramus and Galland, Platonism and Aristotelianism, but proceeds to deal with the woodcutter's
lost axe (Prologue de l'Auteur, Q. L.). Equally clear
when Aristotle[2] is made responsible for Entelechie's
strangenesses, and for the false knowledge of those
employed in recording his discoveries in the Pays de
Satin[3]; when his nature observation is quoted as a
guarantee that sheep will follow a leader (Q. L. 8);
and when the authority of Averroes affirms that a
monk is attracted towards the kitchen (Q. L. 11)[4].
We need not enquire whether in every instance
justification of Rabelais' statements may be found in

[1] Thus even Panurge denounces the testimony of Pro-
pertius, Tibullus, etc.: 'Ilz furent folz comme poetes, et
resveurs comme philosophes' (T. L. 18).
[2] Whose *Ethics* he knew but did not use, see G. 10.
[3] 'En un coing là prés vismes Aristoteles tenant une lanterne
...espiant, considerant, le tout redigeant par escrit. Derriere
luy estoient comme records de sergents plusieurs aultres philosophes,' etc. One of whom '*remained fifty-eight years contemplating the conditions of bees without doing anything else*' (*Quint
Livre*, 31). It would seem that even Rabelais' scientific devotion
would not suffice for that: perhaps he was too concerned with
the human aspects of scientific study. See later chapter.
[4] Other smaller points are: Alexander appears unnecessarily
timid (T. L. 16); Herodotus on primitive speech is scoffed at
(*ibid.* 19); and Epistemon's frequent indications of deceptions
(*ibid.* 24).

the works of this or that author. It is possible that
they are examples of Rabelaisian absurdities—as they
seem to be; and that would only the more definitely
prove that he had changed his intentions. Rabelais
certainly admired Plutarch. He was certainly much
indebted to his works. Yet he did not spare even that
important worker. Plutarch had been guilty of dis-
seminating false knowledge, and all his admirable
work could not save him. 'Henceforth,' says Rabelais
severely to his readers, 'be more ready to believe what
Plutarch assures you he has tested. If a flock of goats
run away at full speed, put a sprig of teazle in the
mouth of the last one as it goes by, and suddenly they
will all stop' (*Q. L.* 62). With harsher ridicule Plato's
thoughts were overwhelmed. 'Ideas' are constantly
contemptuously treated by the obstinate realist. In an
episode destined to help the cismontane cause (*Q. L.*
50), by means of an ingenious and powerful inversion,
the Pope's image figured as the Idea of 'God upon
earth'; so too the hideous monster, porcine and winged,
that hovered over the Andouilles (*Q. L.* 42) was the
Idea of Mardigras; and above all Ideas were depicted
in one of the Medamothi paintings[1], an allusion which
must have *lost* point as art became more and more

---

[1] The pictures were of Echo, Plato's Ideas, Epicurus'
Atoms, and Philomela and Tereus. Of the most probable subject Rabelais says we must not expect a realistic picture. 'Cela
est trop sot et trop lourd. La peincture estoit bien aultre et plus
intelligible. Vous la pourrez voir en Thelème, a main gauche,
entrans en la haulte galerie.' Cp. p. 78.

symbolical. Moreover, the coarse[1] Ennasin episode
becomes intelligible only when we interpret the
'strange alliances' as being between Platonist affinities, and the whole scene as a pseudo-commonwealth
based on the principles of the *Republic* and the
Symposium. The ordinary ties of blood are neglected
as completely as Plato had ever demanded, and the
various contracting parties are such perfect affinities
that the wholes are incomplete and useless without
either separate part. Finally, colonels Riflandouille[2]
and Tailleboudin the Younger were chosen to lead
the attack on the Andouilles, and Epistemon's chance
recollection of good omens in men of such names
produced the inevitable discussion on the significance
of names. In following that debate, in which history
ancient and modern was ransacked for instances, we
almost lose sight of the author's arbitrariness, and like
Rhizotome are almost persuaded to read the *Cratylus*
since Pantagruel so frequently refers to it. We too are
almost persuaded until disillusionment comes upon us,
and so deep a disillusionment that the author pretends
to judge it well to protest against his readers' losing
faith in him[3]. The manner is certainly more intricate,

[1] The later Rabelais usually relapsed into offensive coarseness
in presence of unreality, see p. 30.
[2] A character in *Pantagruel* (p. 97) on the side of Loupgarou.
See pp. 45–6.
[3] 'Vous truphez icy, beuveurs, et ne croyez que ainsi soit en
verite comme je vous raconte. Je ne scaurois que vous en faire.
Croyez le, si voulez; si ne voulez, allez y voir. Mais je scay bien
ce que je vis. Ce fut en l'isle Farouche. Je la vous nomme'
(*Q. L.* 38).

but the purpose is the same as in the *Tiers Livre*.
Throughout his later work Rabelais did more than
attack his Platonist contemporaries[1].

Yet this is not the whole truth. The author's
solemnest moments are those in which his thought
so closely resembles the well-known utterances of the
Dialogues that at first unacknowledged borrowing
may appear to be the only adequate explanation. There
are, however, important if minor divergences. When
Pantagruel's party approached the Isle of Rascals
(Ganabin, *Q. L.* 66), in spite of Xenomanes' promise
of things beautiful to behold ('la plus belle fontaine
du monde, et autour une bien grande forest[2]), they
decided not to land. They decided, however, not
from fear of the thieves, which was Panurge's state,
but wholly because Pantagruel felt an urgent 'movement' in his soul[3] as if a far-off voice had cried to him
that they should not go ashore. Every time that he had

---

[1] Note also Rondibilis' advice (*T. L.* 31-3) in which first
the *old* Platonists' five means of self-restraint are mentioned,
then the medical and anatomical evidence is considered, and
finally a moral solution of the problem is advanced. Thus
Rabelais persisted in the belief that more remained to discover
than what the Ancients had discovered.

[2] Rabelais seems to have delighted in wild scenery. Cp.
Isle de Cassade 'vraye idee de Fontainebleau.'

[3] 'Je sens, dist Pantagruel, en mon ame retraction urgente,
comme si fust une voix de loing ouie, laquelle me dit que ny
debvons descendre. Toutes et quantesfois quen mon esprit jay
tel mouvement senty, je me suis trouve en heur refusant et
laissant la part dont il me retiroit, au contraire en heur pareil
me suis trouve, suivant la part quil me poussoit; et jamais ne
men repenty.—Cest, dist Epistemon, comme le demon de
Socrates tant celebre entre les Academicques' (*Q. L.* 66).

been so moved, moreover, he had been alike fortunate
whether he refused to do what the voice forbade, or
did what it commanded. Up to this time Pantagruel
had been acknowledged supreme in all that belongs
to the thought of the Ancients, and Epistemon had
been excessively careful of exact references. Consequently since Pantagruel does not, and Epistemon
actually does, draw our attention to the resemblance
to the Socratic demon, we may not unjustly infer
that we are probably concerned with an original
observed fact. The *Apologia* definitely states that, unlike the intuitive element in this passage, the voice
never urged Socrates to act[1], yet the author and
observer gladly compares his phenomenon with the
greater example. Impressed by the passage during
his studies, Rabelais had been led by doubt of classical
truth to challenge the facts, but his observation of
himself had half confirmed the truth of Plato, and
fully confirmed that of the *Memorabilia*. In a somewhat similar delicate manner he refused to dispute
Socrates' noble thought, that death in itself was not
evil nor to be feared, even while death in any form,
but specially death by shipwreck, seemed most terrible
to his life-loving nature. 'Ores, si chose est en ceste
vie a craindre apres l'offense de Dieu, je ne veulx
dire que soit la mort. Je ne veulx entrer en la dispute
de Socrates et des academicques. . . . Je dis ceste espece

---

[1] The well-known passage in the *Memorabilia* (Bk I. i. 4)
would confirm Rabelais' critical attitude.

de mort par naufrage estre, ou rien nestre a craindre'
(*Q. L.* 22). A drowning man's helplessness horrified
him; Panurge's abject terror could half win his
sympathy; and, called to his aid on a sudden con-
frontation with his horror, philosophy offered him
her consolations in vain. When reality or his personal
convictions came into conflict with the most sublime
and admirable thought that he knew, he could no
longer depend upon his reverence for authority,
although he could admire the thinkers. When reality
or experience disproved the assertions of ancient
authors, he brushed their work aside. We shall not
therefore misjudge him when we add that he seems
to have tentatively accepted Plato's psychogony.
Little in his experience could be brought to bear
upon the matter, but the mystery in good men's, in
heroes' deaths[1] caused him to seek to divest death of
its terrors, and to depict it as the portal through which
the dying man passed to a troubleless existence among
angels, heroes and good spirits[2]. Before this visit to
the Macreons, which is wholly concerned with the
deaths of superior men, he had observed dying men

[1] References to Guillaume du Bellay's death occur both in
Q. L. 27 and *T. L.* 21, the two outstanding passages in which
the subject is treated of. It seems, therefore, probable that this
impressive incident in Rabelais' life caused him to 'visit' the
old Macrobe (the Ancients) in quest of certainty.
[2] The similarity of Rabelais' belief to Christian immortality
need not be pointed out, but such a combination of ancient
and Christian thought is found only in this connection. It is
a proof of how strongly the problem dominated his mind.

like Raminagrobis (*T. L.* 21), and had hoped to
obtain prophecies of future events; he had noted the
old reformer poet's calmness in face of his end; but
the question does not appear to have been so acute
with him as later it became. To Friar John, the man
of commonplace views, the old Macrobe's assertion,
that heroes and demigods also finally die, seemed
incredible, and he asked Pantagruel for more light
on the subject. Stoical theories of universal mortality
except in the case of the Immortals and the In-
visible, and the various opinions of ancient thinkers
proving inacceptable[1], Pantagruel's personal belief
was forced from him. Thus the personal problem, that his knowledge of his patron's life and
death started up, seems to have led Rabelais to a
study of what the Ancients had to teach him. Most
of ancient philosophy, however, he had felt unable
to accept, and he had concluded, with Plato, that
since life is so incomplete and so liable to be cut short,
there must be a hereafter or the existence of great
men would be incomprehensible. And in somewhat
the same way as he came to Pantagruel's profession
of faith in immortality[2], he adopted without doubt
the account of Pan's death from Plutarch. In *Gar-*

---

[1] He quotes Pindar, Callimachus, Pausanias and Hesiod.
Friar John answers: 'Cela nest poinct matiere de breviaire. Je
n'en croy sinon ce que vous plaira' (*Q. L.* 27).

[2] 'Je croy dist Pantagruel que toutes ames intellectives sont
exemptes des cizeaux de Atropos. Toutes sont immortelles:
anges, demons et humaines.'

gantua, it will be recalled, Friar John had spoken with indignant scorn of the cowardly disciples who abandoned their Master, and we need not be surprised that, rather than orthodox belief, Rabelais' humanity (combined with a passage from his reading) inspired this later chapter, in which his meaning is explicitly stated and which culminates in Pantagruel's emotion and the company's awe. Yet he is not seeking confirmation of Christian tenets among pagan authors. The old disciple of Lucian was sincerely affected by his meditations[1]. He must first have experienced the emotion that his words evoke, and then have adapted a similar passage from his reading. As we have seen, in most cases he seems to have done no more than seek confirmation of his feelings and convictions among the books of his library; and his opinion was that we must study the Ancients with the utmost caution; surely a novelty in his life and a sign of his superiority to his fellows.

His interest in nature-study must early have allowed of his checking off the facts of Pliny's *Natural History* with greater ease than in other authors. As we have noted, he denounced this authority in *Gargantua*, but he borrowed largely from him

[1] This chapter is a remarkable instance of Rabelais' indulgence in nonsense immediately following on some serious passage (cp. pp. 34–5). The passage concludes with: 'Peu de temps apres, nous vismes les larmes decouler de ses œilz grosses comme œufz d'austruche. Je me donne a Dieu si j'en mens d'un seul mot' (*Q. L.* 28).

throughout his career. Thus he relied considerably upon Pliny's account of hemp for the remarkably long passage on Pantagruelion[1], and it has been somewhat rashly concluded that, since a store of hemp was necessary for a long sea voyage, the meaning is simple and clear. Nevertheless the close association with Pantagruel, the explanation that all civilized arts were derived from Pantagruelion's miraculous powers[2], and the striking allusions to burnings, seem to foreshadow quite another meaning, one *deliberately* abstruse and important. For the moment Rabelais' reason for choosing this passage rather than any other must be put aside, but we must remember that the theme of much of the *Tiers Livre* had aroused in his mind all his sexual knowledge. The book is mainly unpleasant because this element so frequently rises to the surface, but since Rondibilis considered that he should enumerate five means whereby Panurge might exercise self-restraint[3] we must accept the problem as scientifically important. There can be

[1] M. Sainéan in a series of articles has traced Rabelais' indebtedness to Pliny ('L'histoire naturelle dans Rabelais,' *R. S. S.* 1916). He has shown the Pantagruelion chapters to consist of (1) direct translation, (2) free rendering, and (3) original matter. It is obvious that those passages containing a free translation are the most critical and important.

[2] This portion was later expanded and emended in the Messer Gaster episode (*Q. L.* 61). It is, therefore, very important.

[3] This is not Panurge's ideal. He also has been consulting the authorities, among them Pliny (*T. L.* 27). Did one search lead to the other?

no doubt that on such a question Rabelais' mind was keenly alive; and his reading would certainly cover and his memory retain all the passages which seemed to be appropriate. The Pantagruelion chapters, associated with chapter 31, would seem to be based on this idea. Thus there occurs the following important passage freely compounded of translation and additions:

However in a man who often eats it and consumes large quantities, it extinguishes the seed of generation. And although formerly among the Greeks they made certain kinds of dishes which they ate as delicacies after supper and in order the better to appreciate their wine, yet it is so difficult to digest that it offends the stomach, engenders bad blood, and by its excess of heat affects the brain and fills the head with troublesome and painful vapours[1].

It is obvious that there is a common idea between this passage and Rondibilis' advice; obvious too that this free rendering could apply *by wilful ambiguity* both to drugs and plants, and to fervent study[2]. Furthermore, the author had slipped into using wine in an allegorical sense, speaking of the 'wine' of his own books; and the certain dishes after supper may

[1] 'Mais estainct en lhomme la semence generative, qui en mangeroit beaucoup et souvent. Et quoy que jadis entre les Grecs d'icelle lon fist certaines especes de fricassees, tartes et bignetz, lesquels ilz mangeoient apres souper par friandise, et pour trouver le vin meilleur, si est-ce quelle est de difficile concoction, offense lestomac, engendre mauvais sang, et par son excessive chaleur ferit le cerveau et remplit la teste de fascheuses et douloureuses vapeurs' (*T. L.* 49).

[2] Rondibilis' other three means of restraint cannot be applied to this passage.

be both literal and a reference to symposia. Now in such a passage the hidden meaning must be fervent study. It is difficult, short of adopting most improbable views on the author of the *Tiers Livre*, to come to any other conclusion. Fervent study applies to the above passage; and it will unravel the extremely difficult chapters that follow surprisingly well. It had produced all the conveniences of civilization enumerated. It could not be repressed by burnings[1]. It might, the author hoped, enable humanity to attain truth to the consternation of the gods[2], although he confesses that he cannot expound all its possibilities ('car le tout est a moy vous exposer impossible'— *T. L.* 50). Undoubtedly, moreover, it was the guiding principle of the new Pantagruel, and surely in their quest of certainty it was more important than ropes. Hemp is as inadequate an explanation of Pantagruelion to which we owe milling, legal practice, building, printing, and geographical discovery[3], as it was certainly the subject of Rabelais' original. Once more, whimsically enough no doubt, Rabelais is seen to have

---

[1] 'Le feu qui tout devore, tout degaste et consume, purge et blanchist ce seul Pantagruelion Carpasien Asbestion' (*T. L.* 52).

[2] Rabelais substituted this concluding passage for a much more moderate conclusion in Pliny.

[3] Cp. *T. L.* 52, where he quotes problems: 'Si j'avois en ceste bouteille mis deux cotyles de vin et une d'eau, ensemble fort bien meslés, comment les demesleriez vous, comment les separeriez vous, de maniere que vous me rendriez leau a part sans le vin, le vin sans leau, en mesure pareille que les y aurois mis?'

resorted to a classical authority for materials where-
with to furbish forth his own conceptions. But the
passage is not yet exhausted. 'I am aghast,' he ex-
claims, 'that the discovery of such a use (for Pantagruelion) has been hidden for so many centuries from
the ancient philosophers' ('Et m'esbahys comment
l'invention de tel usaige a este par tant de siècles celé
aux antiques philosophes'—*T. L.* 51). Possibly the
Pays de Satin was this modernist's reply to such a
query; but certainly, as so frequently happened with
Rabelais' cherished ideas, this preliminary hint found
repetition, amplification and particular application, in
Bacbuc's farewell speech. 'Your philosophers,' she
said to the departing travellers, 'who complain that
everything has been written by the Ancients and that
nothing has been left for them to discover, are only
too obviously mistaken' ('vos philosophes, qui se
complaignent toutes choses estre par les anciens
escrites, rien ne leur estre laissé a inventer, ont tort
trop evident'—*Quint Livre*, 48).

These then are the utterances and visions of a man
who apparently felt that the widest of gaps separated
him from his contemporaries[1], who appreciated their
inevitable weakness in that they were fast bound by
tradition, and whose whole life from a certain time
was occupied, we cannot doubt, with urging his

---

[1] Cp. *T. L.* 50, where he refers to many modern Pantagruelists whose method of preparing Pantagruelion is repre-
hensible.

fellows to undertake independent activities. Such a man must have largely freed himself from the shackles of the past. As we have seen, save in the all-important, because personal, perplexity of human destiny which, after his utmost independent reflection, had forced him back upon authoritative and traditional views, his works afford evidence of considerable independence. Classical authority had been weighed in the balances of experience[1],—that was the surest guide,—and found wanting in many respects. The visionary who foresaw human progress could no longer, like others, try to 'live his life backwards,' but must push forward like Pantagruel into certainty. The transformation of the Platonist must have resulted from his experiences between 1535 and 1546, and, if we may surmise that his unacknowledged borrowings prove that he addressed himself to an un-learned audience, it is important because thereby he would influence the growing class of bourgeois, that class from which those kindred spirits, La Fontaine and Molière, were to spring.

[1] Notice specially that while Epistemon matched one authority against another, Pantagruel relied upon his reason and common experience.

6. THE QUESTION OF RELIGION

IN a former chapter the subject of Rabelais' religion has been already touched upon. We saw there that in all probability an intimate friend believed that he could trace in the author of *Gargantua's* conversation proofs of most dangerous infidelity; so much so indeed that he seems to have torn himself free from so dangerous a friend. We saw too that Calvin himself regarded Rabelais as one who 'having tasted the gospel had been struck with spiritual blindness.' Unfortunately we may not in this modern age be guided in our present search by such conclusions. For us it would be perhaps impossible to sympathize with the religious beliefs either of Voulté or of Calvin. We probably no longer hold the same faith as they, and if we accept Calvin as a modern Protestant, Voulté as a modern Catholic, we shall inevitably be misled in appreciating Rabelais' true position. At the present time Protestantism and Catholicism have by a gradual and insensible progress modified their standards, and without some brief consideration of the general religious conceptions of the time it is impossible to place Rabelais in his historical position and even to appreciate the religious feeling of his romance.

The outstanding feature of that epoch was the nearly universal concern with theological matters. At least during the earlier half of the sixteenth century not merely schools of divinity but homes resounded with religious debate, and, after the decisive emergence of Calvinism (sharply differentiated as it was) and the consequent persecution, an extensive and well-organized system of colportage, which smuggled tracts and sermons into France and disseminated them there, maintained the interest though necessarily in closely guarded circles. Those tracts were passed from hand to hand in the greatest secrecy, and all the charms of conspiracy were added to the fierce enough discussions, since, as Rabelais says, 'men are always tempted to seek out things forbidden' ('Car nous entreprenons tousjours choses defendues, et convoitons ce que nous est denié'—G. 57[1]). Indeed were it not for the rise to power[2] of the *Politiques*, with their patriotic disregard for religious zeal, which dates historically from about the time of our author's death, we might legitimately suspect that the spread of Huguenot resistance and the religious wars prove the non-abatement of this earlier enthusiasm. Resort to violence has probably in all times been the sign of a diminishing rather than of a sustained interest, since when the former power over men's minds has been lost, the weakening party has sought to compel

[1] Later, and in a manner easily understood, the unscrupulous author of the *Tiers Livre* applied this general maxim to the *particular* case of women (*T. L.* 34), but this apparently was forced upon him by the companions' free comments upon Rondibilis' fable.

[2] See their powerful manifesto in *La Satire Ménippée*, which, be it noted in passing, betrays some Rabelaisian influence.

where it had found unhesitating submission; and apart from Calvin's unanimity with Catholics in persecutions like that of Servetus, there were many indications of the definite abatement in theological interest. Montaigne noted, as the characteristic feature of his day, an 'execrable atheism' or rather an ever-increasing apathy in religious matters and a tendency to presume to judge of questions without being adequately equipped for judgment. His opinion must be well weighed and, if accepted, accepted with caution. He appears to have maintained that, since our reason is most fallible, we must in religion fall back upon custom and the practice of our forefathers, which must be enforced at need by all the power and authority of ecclesiastical and political institutions since freedom of enquiry would certainly lead to critical speculations upon those institutions them-selves[1]. To Montaigne the Church seemed principally to act as the buttress of the State, and therefore only those modern peoples, who have failed to penetrate to the true inwardness of religion, may accept his standards. We need not, and indeed cannot, suppose that this view was wide-spread, but the insistence upon the need for authority links it up both with early Calvinism and with Catholicism. The very freedom

[1] 'Le vulgaire, n'ayant pas la faculté de juger les choses par elles-mesmes, se laissant emporter à la fortune et aux apparences ...il jecte...toutes les impressions qu'il avoit receues par l'auto-rité des loix ou reverence de l'ancien usage' (*Apologie de Raimond Sebond*, Essais, II. 12).

which had been the starting point of his work Calvin strove to repress when his creed really came into existence, and the main difference between Montaigne's position and that of Calvin is that, whereas the former urged anti-rational arguments, the latter tried to rationalize the belief in the Supernatural. 'New presbyter was but old priest writ large.'

Considered from this point of view, if we had no more than the well-known account of Thelema, the challenge to classical authority and his mature tolerance of national institutions, Rabelais' religious principles would probably elude the clearest eyes. In Thelema he would seem to have abolished ecclesiastical authority just as Protestantism has been since prone to do, and his doubts on the real function of ancient literature would support any subversive tendencies; but his manifest mature disinclination to tamper with the pillars of the State must make us pause and consider. We feel sure however that, on this question of justifying religion by the conservation of older manners, Rabelais could not have subscribed either to the Calvinist or the Catholic tenet. Was he therefore necessarily opposed to Christianity? Long before the new church was fully organized, Rabelais' life had closed, and his work falls into those years of struggle and debate during which Calvin shifted his ground from that of a moderate reformer and iconoclast to the head of a strictly logical hierarchy; during which, too, Marguerite of Angoulême strove vainly to adapt revealed religion and Platonist philosophy together[1], unaware of the harm she did to both, and mainly seeking to reconcile her two authorities; and during which civil and ecclesiastical dignitaries united in one condemnation both new sectarians and students of letters. The task becomes the more difficult, and the problem only soluble by a consideration of one of the chief features of religious practice.

Catholicism, based upon Holy Church authority as confirmed by the canonical books and by patristic writings, had extended that foundation, by processes of absorption and accretion, over vast fields of specula-tion, of 'hear-say' knowledge (*ouy-dire*) and dis-torted nature observation[2] such as we now commonly regard as superstitions. The faith has now so gradually justified itself by rejection of one article after another that we can hardly believe in our ancestors' sincere faith in *succubi* and *loupgarou*, in witches and demoniacal possession: we find such beliefs monstrous and incredible; our very language, preserving the names, has betrayed us somewhat. They appear how-ever to have formed an integral part of Church teaching, to have been universally accepted for centuries, and to have driven even moderate men to

[1] Like the Florentine attempt, a century earlier, doomed to failure.
[2] Cp. Cellini's beliefs as described in his *Autobiography* and explained by J. A. Symonds in the Introduction to his edition; also the numerous *Bestiaires*, etc., of the Middle Ages.

most inhuman cruelties[1]. In vain did humanitarians oppose the inquisitorial activities. In vain were the arguments for and against belief in witches marshalled in equally imposing volumes. The most varied, the most acute minds were alike obsessed with the belief. The acknowledged task of all true Christians was with the Crusader's zeal to extirpate the agents of the Evil One; and in opposition reason was of little avail because, in the accepted and acceptable form of ancient philosophy, ample confirmation was to be found, when needed, for all their speculations. Mankind was dominated by good and evil supernatural beings who thwarted or cherished its most natural aspirations. Logical grounds abounded in the learning of the day, and, though we might have expected some growth of scepticism with the freer study of ancient originals, the ceremonies of the Church (especially those placatory of offended Powers) were so intermingled with superstitions that, when at last frenzied reformers insulted the Mass in 1534, people and clergy, students and moderate reformers united in demanding the punishment of the malefactors. It was everybody's duty to put aside minor differences in order by burning pyres to placate the offended deity. It must be apparent that, at that time, to disbelieve in witchcraft and superstition required that man should challenge the premiss that this universe comprised natural and supernatural

[1] Lecky, *History of Rationalism*, vol. I, p. 7.

beings; or that he should have so little religious feeling that he lived merely for the sensual and the gross. Neither Luther nor Erasmus threw off this dualistic view. Certainly the logical Calvin was not only personally incapable of taking so vast a stride forward, but, as Lecky pointed out, even his faith, preserved in its greatest purity, has longest maintained the belief in witchcraft. Having denied the Church's infallibility, but reserving to ordained teachers the right of interpretation[1], Calvin offered no greater freedom to the individual than orthodoxy did, and his fulminatory tracts and sermons reveal a sincere belief in much that the Church also upheld. He asserted that to doubt the existence of Evil Powers is to doubt that of the Good, upon which religion itself is founded, and he supported this contention with numerous Biblical texts. He denounced the growing belief that there may be a spiritual explanation of such conceptions as the devil, the world, and sin[2], and in very fact the men of Calvin's generation, who reverent of all authority believed in the literal truth of the Scriptures, could hardly help bowing their

[1] Cp. Rabelais' picture of Hippothadée, *T. L.* 30.

[2] 'Quaeret igitur hic aliquis quae sit eorum opinio de diabolo. Respondeo, ipsos eum nominare et de eo loqui sed more suo et sensu. Diabolum enim, mundum et peccatum accipiunt pro imaginatione, quae nihil est....Nec solum de diabolo loquuntur ut de Angelis, censentes ipsos esse inspirationes essentia vacuas: sed aiunt vanas esse cogitationes, quae, veluti somnia, oblivione obruenda sunt.' *Instructio adversus fanaticam ac furiosam sectam libertinorum qui se spirituales vocant*, 1544.

heads before 'a great number of evil-doing gods, imagined by poets' ('comme les poetes feignent un grand tas de Vejoves et dieux malfaisants'—*G.* 45[1]). And although this Rabelaisian utterance of years before must not be overstrained it may be admitted that to doubt the existence of the Powers of Evil implied no uncertain scepticism as to the others. Therefore Rabelais' scornful rejection of the devil and all his works must weigh considerably in our estimate of his religious beliefs.

In the *Quint Livre* occurs a passage which might serve as an illustration of one of Rabelais' governing principles. The travellers are discussing the *Frères Fredons*, and the remark of one that 'their subtlety is extracted from occult philosophy and is utterly incomprehensible' draws from Pantagruel the reply:

It is all the more to be feared because we understand nothing of it. For subtlety that is understood, anticipated and laid bare, loses all its subtlety, both its essence and its name, and we name it stupidity ('finesse entendeue, finesse preveue, finesse descouverte, perd de finesse et l'essence et le nom, nous la nommons lourderie'—*Quint Livre*, 27).

It is to be remarked, as we have seen above, that the task of the *Tiers Livre* was probably just this, to unmask and ridicule various impostures in human life. Before that time Rabelais had written contemptuously of the supernatural: he had described Loupgarou's destruction by Pantagruel (*P.* p. 96) and he had vividly

[1] Many a truth spoken in jest. Rabelais speaks of pagan literature.

and feelingly reported Epistemon's regret at being
called back from Hell (*P.* pp. 98–102)[1]; but these
are perhaps little more than the coarse reckless
extravagances that medieval imaginations found so
amusing, and that the priests themselves possibly
encouraged[2]. They do not prove that Rabelais was
not perfectly orthodox. Nor did Grandgousier's attack
upon priestly doctrines (*G.* 45) prove that he intended
any disrespect to the real power of Saints who might
punish remissness with plagues. At the most the
benevolent king doubts whether such holy men would
in fact do what was evil to their worshippers, and he
treats shrines and pilgrimages much more tolerantly
than Erasmus' *Colloquia* had done. What Grandgousier
attacks is not the power of the Saints but the priests'
unscrupulousness. It is later in the work that
Rabelais appears earnestly and unrestingly to have
aimed at sapping the power of the supernatural over
men's minds, and in its place to try to substitute a
cheerful, if not a joyous, scepticism[3]. The terrors of
the interview with the Sibyl of Panzoust are almost
forgotten in amusement at Panurge's grotesque fears,
contrasted with Epistemon's calmness; and before the
appearance of that notable necromancer, Her Trippa

[1] 'Et asseuroit devant tous, que les diables estoyent bons
compaignons.'
[2] Cp. the treatment of the devil in Morality and Miracle
plays.
[3] Nevertheless sufficient of the coarser jesting is to be found
to justify Voulté's and Calvin's mistrust.

is mocked unmercifully because he had been unable to foresee his marriage disasters. It was the comically perplexed and credulous Panurge who came forward as the appropriate exponent of the 'diabolology of Toledo,' and still later the Evil One himself was to be outwitted by an old peasant-woman's ingenuity. True, only a little and inexperienced devil could be so deceived, and only in a story of the old *fabliau* variety, but the inference is no less sound for all the coarseness[1]. His treatment of the theme is elsewhere more intricately bound up with the story: thus the Raminagrobis episode is marked by the subtle suggestion that there was a close alliance between friars and devils, and their mutual relations were confused by Panurge (*T. L.* 23)[2]; and Panurge's excessive zeal in offering to relieve Friar John of his money, lest the crosses thereon should provoke the devils to most outrageous violence as they carried him off, must have stirred thrifty bourgeois to peals of laughter, and so have calmed minds which supernatural terror dominated (*ibid.*). Furthermore there occur assurances that the devil assumes the shapes of perverse advocates, counsellors and procureurs (*T. L.* 44); that he sups on the agents of abuses (*Q. L.* 46); and

[1] See above, p. 30, for an explanation of Rabelais' mature use of coarseness.
[2] Cp. *A. P.*, where the author describes his enemies and devils: 'Car, en grec, calomnie est dicte diabole....Je les nomme diables noirs, diables blancs...ces nouveaulx diables engipponés,' etc.

finally, in work prudently left unpublished, and because the legal profession had been a main prop of superstitions, that all the supposedly inexplicable disasters, commonly attributed to the Powers of Evil, should be attributed to the wickedness of the Furry Cats:

And if at any time occur in the world plagues, famines or wars, earthquakes or horrors, conflagrations or any other form of misfortune, do not attribute or refer them to conjunctions of evil planets, to the abuses of the Roman Court, to the tyranny of earthly kings and princes, ... nor to the perversity of adulterous and lustful women who murder their children, but attribute the whole to the enormous, unspeakable wickedness that is constantly forged and used in the Furry Cats' sanctum, and that is no more known to mankind than the Jewish cabbala.

Certainly the passage reads extravagant; indeed it appears probable that the writer wished to produce somewhat of the same extraordinary terror as superstitions did; but what is more to the purpose is that he substituted for a vague unknown cause of evils one that could be verified by his readers, and, what is more, one amenable to reform, and that will be reformed, he goes on to say, as soon as the evil influence is recognized[1].

<hr/>

[1] 'De ce quelque jour vous souuienne, et si jamais pestes au monde, famines, guerres, horraiges, cataglismes, conflagrations, ou autre malheur advient, ne l'attribuez ne le referez aux conionctions des planettes maleficques, aux abus de la court Rommaine, aux tyrannies des roys et princes terriens...a la perversité des femmes adulteres, venefiques, infanticides, attribuez le tout a l'enorme, indicible, incroyable, et inestimable

These indirect attacks upon the upholders of the
beliefs, the religious hierarchy and the law, are however less powerful than certain episodes of which the
only explanation appears to be a good-natured tolerance of his readers' prejudices. Repeatedly he seems
to create monsters which closely resemble supernatural beings, only to demonstrate their essential
unreality; or he paints realistic pictures of effects
particularly associated with the operations of magic.
To the reader's mind will occur transformations into
birds (*Isle Sonante*) and into cats, papal bulls with
mysterious powers over French gold, and Pantagruelion, the virtues of which, proved by actual experiment, far transcend those of the more commonplace
wonders revealed by medieval science. Supreme however above all others tower the tutelary Mardigras
and the persecuting Quaresmeprenant[1], respectively

meschanceté, laquelle est continuellement forgee et exercee en
l'officine des chats fourrez: et ne est du monde congnue non
plus que la caballe des Juifs. Pour autant n'est elle corrigee,
detestee et reprimee comme seroit de raison. Mais si elle est
quelque jour mise en evidence et manifestee au peuple. Il n'est
et ne fut Orateur tant eloquent qui par son art le retint, ny loy
tant rigoureuse et draconique, qui par crainte de peine le
gardast, ne magistrat tant puissant qui par force l'empeschast
de les faire tous vifs dedans leurs raboutieres felonnement brusler
leurs enfans propres chatz fourrillons et autres parens les
auroient en horreur et abomination,' *I. S.* pp. 25–6. Compare,
for identifications, Lecky, *History of Rationalism*, vol. I, ch. I.
Note the commonly accepted notions of poisoners, *succubi*,
incendiaries, and the general evil influence through the Jews.

[1] Of Quaresmeprenant, Xenomanes says: 'Nous en oyrons
par adventure plus amplement parler passans l'isle Farouche,

worshipped and dreaded by the poor Andouilles. Their powers over the Andouillic race are those of gods[1] and devils over humanity, and although the little people might seem to have little in common with man except comic ferocity, suspicious natures and very human fears, yet in the change from stout resistance to abject terror when they think that they recognize the malevolent principle of their universe we must perhaps see human beings trembling before the Powers of Evil so long as the menace hangs over them[2]. And in order that this parallel should not be overlooked, Rabelais took pains to discuss at some length the importance of these creatures to mankind, and the passage rapidly degenerated into his semi-delusive nonsense (*Q. L.* 38). We must here add that Mardigras was left comparatively vague[3], that he was in a measure respected; while Quaresmeprenant had as a preliminary been anatomically described by Xenomanes and shown to be an impossible being

en laquelle dominent les Andouilles farfelues, ses ennemies mortelles, contre lesquelles il a guerre sempiternelle. Et ne fust l'aide du noble Mardigras, leur protecteur et bon voisin, ce grand lanternier Quaresmeprenant les eust ja piéça exter-minées de leur manoir' (*Q. L.* 29).

[1] 'Niphleseth respondit que c'est l'idée de Mardigras, leur dieu tutelaire en temps de guerre, premier fondateur et original de toute la race andouillicque. Pourtant sembloit il a un pourceau, car andouilles furent de pourceau extraictes' (*Q. L.* 42).

[2] Note, however, a reference to the Council of Chesil (Trent) which restored the hostility between Quaresmeprenant and the Andouilles (*Q. L.* 35).

[3] The *Idea* of Mardigras was described as a big hog, cp. n. 1.

compounded of all that was monstrous, impossible and revolting (*Q. L.* 30–2), a thing that reminded Pantagruel of the children of Antiphysie[1]. Rabelais would seem to suggest that man's fears in the supernatural world might, on a similar analysis, prove to be equally impossible and composed of equally incongruous elements. Many of Rabelais' monsters are of the same type: the good Bringuenarilles may devour windmills, he may oppress humanity, but 'he died strangled sitting in the chimney corner as he ate a little fresh butter by doctor's orders.' The moment such monsters are treated naturally and rationally they cease to trouble mankind.

Were it possible further to doubt Rabelais' intense hatred of superstitions and his persistent optimism, his utterances on the subject of comets and other celestial and terrestrial phenomena would set the matter beyond dispute. Naturally he did not succeed in reaching anything like modern scientific views, indeed he could not offer a reasoned opinion[2], but he did avoid a gloomy interpretation. Apparently he entirely lacked sympathy with that contemporary speculation which represented these sights as proofs of God's displeasure and which maintained its hold on mankind to a much later day. In his discussion on the deaths of heroes, occasioned in Rabelais' mind

[1] Among whom are 'the demoniacal Calvins, imposters of Geneva.' Calvin also supported the belief.
[2] He seems to have had recourse to classical lore.

probably by Guillaume du Bellay's death, the Macrobe is made to say:

We believe since the comet, which appeared to us for the three preceding days, is no longer shining, that one of those heroes is dead, and his death has excited the horrible storm that you have suffered; for, during their life, every good thing abounds in this place and other neighbouring islands, and at sea there is constant calm and good weather. On the death of any one of them ordinarily we hear from the forest great pitiful lamentations and we see on earth plagues, accidents and troubles; in the air darkness and storm, and at sea tempest (*Q. L.* 26).

This Pantagruel translates into comprehensible *human* terms: while heroes live their lives are peaceful, useful, delightful and honourable, and when they die there occur changes in religion, and disturbances in State affairs. Phenomena on land and sea are as by a kind of cosmic sympathy caused by human lamentations, but particularly comets are warning signs given by the skies of the hero's approaching death. Like prudent doctors warning relatives of their dying patients' conditions,

the kindly heavens, in their joy at the approaching reception of those blessed souls, seem to light bonfires in those comets and meteoric phenomena, and they wish human beings to accept them as a very sure prophecy that within a few days certain venerable souls will quit their bodies and the earth[1].

[1] 'Les cieulx benevoles, comme joyeux de la nouvelle reception de ces beates ames, avant leur deces semblent faire feux de joye par telz cometes et apparitions metéores. Lesquelles voulent les cieulx estre aux humains pour pronostic certain et veridicque prediction que, dedans peu de jours, telles venerables ames laisseront leurs corps et la terre' (*Q. L.* 27).

The passage with its almost certain personal bearing probably referred to Rabelais' distresses after his patron's death in particular, but it had a wider scope and upon the minds of most of his readers its effect must have been to induce more pleasant reflections than were customary.

Rabelais, then, ridiculed belief in the Powers of Evil. He had essayed calling them into being and analyzing them. He professed his faith in a supreme benevolent principle. Again and again, and in various ways (except argumentation), he struggled against humanity's obsessions, probably because he had found his enquiries obstructed by them. It is easy to slip into apathy while the universe appears to be the prey of two rival all-powerful forces. Faced with the awe-inspiring horror of the Frozen Words[1], Pantagruel—and therefore Rabelais—insisted upon enquiring into the mystery while the credulous Panurge trembled helplessly. There is an attractive, but perhaps a too modern, speculation that Pantagruel and Panurge represent two aspects of the author's personality, but all the more honour would be due to him in that hypothesis because this episode would demonstrate his will to reject the superficial mystery of things. We may then conclude that in this respect Rabelais found himself shut out, or shut himself out, from communion with both the main branches of Christianity,

[1] Q. L. 55–6. A difficult episode which may be a representation of the Renaissance.

as well as from that of Protestants like Erasmus who maintained their faith in a somewhat less crude form.

Only by studying Rabelais' religion in the light of these most consistent and undoubting principles, does it seem possible to avoid the confusion of mind implied in interpreting him variously as an ardent Protestant, as a moderate Reformer and as the restorer of an enlightened Paganism. Only thereby may we be prepared to find that in this as in other respects his mature views were probably considerably nearer to ours than to those of his contemporaries. From a partial study of his work, from a study or emphasis of either section, any one of those opinions may be formed; from a study of the whole work it may be seen that what remained fairly constant, what was dictated by his thoughts and views of man and not by fashions of the day, developed in his latest work, as his attacks on superstition developed, to something quite different. We must remember that the religious utterances of the first two books were those of a man necessarily inexperienced in the world, and consequently unskilled in the examination of his inner processes, while the remainder express his riper opinions. We must recall that at that time reform of the Church, pressed for in varying degrees by the orthodox (even by the Pope Paul III himself), men of letters, and reformers, was 'in the air,' and that his immediate circle included enthusiastic Platonists.

We must above all consider not merely the Abbey of Thelema which at first sight appears to advocate complete liberty of conscience, nor even merely Gargantua's few 'reformist' outbursts, but in addition we must study the earlier *Pantagruel* which in so many respects will invalidate such *ex parte* conclusions. It is impossible to suppose that sympathy with reform, which finds utterance in one book only, should be strongly felt by the author of those books. Nay, even the profession of a creed need not be strong evidence of real religious faith at à time when externalism passed muster as sincere belief. It is when we discover his perplexities and his tentative explanations, above all when unprotected and alone he treated of religious matters, that we may feel and emphatically declare that at last we have the real man, actively concerned with questions of such moment.

A religious element in *Pantagruel* (1533) may perhaps be explained only by the contemporary fascination of theology. Comparisons of that book with *Gargantua* will however show that changes took place even in that respect; that these changes correspond to those which we may postulate in the author's circumstances, and that therefore we must conclude that the changes in his religious views were in a measure forced upon him. He changed his utterances as he changed his public. Of personal feeling for religion there is little or none,—his experience had deprived him of that, and modern readers, who attempt to bring the adventures narrated into harmony with religion, will succeed only in realizing the peculiar religious temper of the time, and Rabelais' full personal accordance with it. So long as religion meant little more than belief in intellectual propositions, the most complete divorce between actions and principle was possible. Gargantua's letter to his son, for example, probably at most reveals some familiarity with the commonplaces of religious conversation[1]; it is such a letter as Rabelais' father himself may have written to his famous son, or even such an one as Rabelais himself might have penned to a son of his. We cannot stress a mention of the Last Judgment which seems to necessitate the concluding phrase, 'when Jesus Christ shall have given up to God the Father his peaceful kingdom' ('quand Jesus-christ aura rendu a Dieu le pere son Royaulme pacificque hors tout dangier et contamination du peche'—p. 24). In such formal phrases the famous letter abounds; they imply little of any lasting value as evidence. But when we examine his meditations

---

[1] *P.* pp. 23-8. Cp. Grandgousier, *G.* 28: 'Bon Dieu, tu cognois mon coraige car a toy rien ne peut estre cele'; *G.* 29: 'Dieu eternel la laisse au gouvernail de *son franc arbitre et propre sens* qui ne peut estre que meschant, si par grace divine nest continuellement guidé' (Hippothadée's method of argument, *T. L.* 30); *G.* 40, where in answer to 'Why has Friar John such a long nose?' he says: 'Par ce qu'ainsi Dieu la voulu,' etc. (Is this a speculation such as offended Voulté?) In striking contrast is the later letter (*Q. L.* 3) in which 'La paix de l'Eternel soit avec toy' stands in almost lonely splendour.

upon a kind of immortality attainable by the propagation of his race, and—alongside the formal
acceptance of the doctrine of original sin—his belief
in the possibility of redemption by man's descendants[1],
we may possibly have to conclude that the definitely
religious utterances betray a nebulousness peculiar
to unskilled theological disputants; *or*, it may be, we
must perceive Rabelais' optimism and his belief in
human nature beginning to pierce his conventional
thought. Certainly we need not hesitate to conclude
that on those points of orthodoxy the writer had no
strong convictions. Naturally at a time when Lefèvre
d'Etaples' enthusiasm was still potent, Pantagruel's
course of study included the Bible in the original
tongues, but the father's wish to see in his son 'an
abyss of learning' (*P.* p. 27) must undoubtedly mean
that, if learning had demanded a choice, Gargantua
would prefer a stupendously learned son to a devout
one. There is no apparent adherence to a definite
creed such as we should expect from a devoted
sectarian or even from a very devout man; and un-

---

[1] 'Entre les dons, graces, et prerogatiues, desquelles le sou-
verain plasmateur Dieu tout puissant a endouayre et aorne
l'humaine nature a son commencement, celle me semble sin-
guliere et excellente, par laquelle elle peult en estat mortel
acquerir une espece de immortalite, et en decours de vie
transitoire perpetuer son nom et sa semence....Dont nous est
aulcunement instaure ce qui nous a este tollu par le peche de noz
premiers parens, esquelz fut dit...quuilz mourroyent....Je ne
me reputeray point totallement mourir, mais plus tost passer
dung lieu en aultre attendu que en toy et par toy je demeure
en mon ymage visible en ce monde...' (*P.* p. 24).

THE QUESTION OF RELIGION 139

doubtedly the young prince made no attempt to put
his father's advice into practice. Uncharitableness,
delight in the things of this world and giving his
heart unto vanity, all of which Gargantua's letter
denounced[1], are the breath and being of the bohemian
adventures that followed. Certainly those stories,
medieval in tone and substance, were unworthy of
a moderate reformer in an age when godless students
were converted by the earnestness of their masters
into godfearing men, and we cannot well avoid the
conclusion that the real Rabelais was hardly touched
by the beginnings of the Reformation, or even by
his knowledge of religion. He (and his readers) per-
ceived no discrepancy between his hero's course of
life and those noble if conventional ideals of conduct.
Pantagruel disregarded the ethical and perhaps adopted
the ritualist advice in erecting a trophy, whereon he
ascribed the victory to learning ('engin mieux vaut
que force') before rendering thanks to God.

For victory, as is well known, depends only on will of the
consistory in which the great Lord reigns in glory; it comes
not to the stronger or the greater, but, as we must believe,

---

[1] 'Sapience nentre point en ame maliuole, Et science sans
conscience nest que ruyne de lame. Il te convient seruir, aymer,
et craindre Dieu, et en luy mettre toutes tes pensees et tout ton
espoir: Et par foy formee de charite estre a luy adjoinct, en
sorte que jamais nen soys desempare par peche, aye suspectz
les Abus du monde; Et ne metz point ton cueur a vanite: car
ceste vie est transitoire: mais la parolle de dieu demeure eternel-
lement. Sois seruiable a tous les prochains, et les ayme comme
toymesmes' (P. pp. 27–8).

to him who is pleasing to God. Then he who hopes by faith in Him has honour and wealth. (Car la victoire | Comme est notoire, | Ne gist que en heur, | Du Consistoire | Ou regne en gloire | Le hault seigneur, | Vient, non au plus fort ou greigneur: | Mais a qui luy plaist, com fault croire: | Donc a et chevance et honneur | Cil qui par foy en luy espoire—*P*. p. 86.)

We need not emphasize the grudging recognition perceptible in 'com fault croire,' but we must point out the notion of actual profit to be obtained by one's faith[1] and the insipidly gross Panurgean parody of which the sole merit is the ingeniousness of the rimes. Pantagruel's prayer in the midst of the battle, such as we find in many heroic stories, and the shocking use of 'Alors fut ouie une voix du ciel' are merely further instances which go to prove either that what religious interest obtains was a literary convention, or that the author could appreciate no Christian feeling[2]. The author either disregarded the claims of religion upon him, or he lacked the elements of religiousness. And the latter is not out of keeping with a life transformed by rebellion against monastic rule. Beyond the monastic ceremonial and exercises, into which he had been forced before his childhood had been spent, he had probably experienced little

[1] Cp. Panurge's address to Dindenault (*Q. L.* 7), and the author's remonstrances to the believers in predestination (*Q. L.* Prol. de l'Auteur), referred to above, for Rabelais' later condemnation of this motive.

[2] Somewhat less shocking is Friar John's remark: 'Les heures sont faictes pour lhomme et non lhomme pour les heures' (*G.*41).

and cared nothing for his experience. And the proof of it lies in that when, in conformity with the ruling fashion, he came to plan a reformed abbey, his hatred of rules proved incompatible with the introduction of religion—even as then understood.

For, unless we make the unwarranted and most improbable assumption that he had conceived the modern ideal of complete liberty of conscience when he wrote *Gargantua*, that splendid institution, Thelema, appears to be least concerned with religion. True, the persons admitted were to be good Christians and Holy Writ was to be studied, he hoped[1], and to each suite of rooms there was a private chapel attached ('chascune garnie de arriere chambre, cabinet, garderobe, chapelle, et issue en une grande salle'—*G.* 53). Apart from this there is no indication that religion, as we understand it, was in the author's mind. The Thelemites spent their days in various worldly activities; and the Abbey really allowed unrestricted opportunities for liberal-minded people of good birth to prosecute their cultured interests. This was probably the author's ideal at that date; and his magnificent motto ('Fais ce que vouldras'), which may or may not reflect an unorthodox belief in human goodness, was quite out

---

[1] La parole Saincte
Ja ne soit extaincte
En ce lieu tres-sainct.
Chascun en soit ceinct;
Chascune ait enceincte
La parole Saincte.   (*G.* 54.)

of harmony with the Christianity of the time[1]. Rabelais certainly did not disapprove of monastic institutions; but he objected most strongly to rules which limited his activity[2], and these considerations, more in harmony with the facts of his life at that time than with advanced idealism, should help us to realize that he was unable to conceive of religion, which must restrain impulses, or even of communal worship. The same vagueness colours the utterances of Grandgousier: he may make the seemingly Protestant remark that priestly intercession for mankind is unnecessary[3], but he too approved of conscientious monks whose labours, like the studies of the Thelemites, would be socially valuable. The idle monk was condemned because, unlike peasants, soldiers, doctors, preachers and merchants, he did nothing for the State. Indeed his praise of Friar John passed the bounds of moderation, as far as the reader may judge, and yet in the monk's eyes it was insufficient.

[1] Critics have selected the Abbey motto in proof of Rabelais' fixed hostility to Christianity.

[2] 'Et par ce que es religion de ce monde, tout est compasse, limite, et reigle par heures, fut decrete que la ne seroit horologe ny quadrant aulcun....Car, disoit Gargantua, le plus vraie perte du temps quil sceust estoit de compter les heures...et la plus grande resverie du monde estoit soy gouverner au son d'une cloche, et non au dicte de bon sens et entendement' (G. 52).

[3] He advises the pilgrims to return home and live as St Paul teaches them, G. 45; and in spite of the remarks on the plague, G. 27 (p. 11, n. 1) he assures them that plague will not trouble them.

'He is not bigoted, nor tattered in his dress; he is honest, merry, and a good companion. He works, he tills the ground; he defends the oppressed, comforts the afflicted, helps the sufferers; he guards the abbey precincts.'—'Nay,' said the monk, 'I do much more. For, as I am getting off our matins and anniversaries by heart, at the same time I make cords for cross-bows, and nets and traps to catch conies' (G. 40).

The man who could thus intermingle the laughable and the serious, even though he meant to satirize monasticism, can hardly be conceived as reverent of holy things. It is impossible to disentangle the two elements; the one seems to have been introduced in order to prepare the way for the other. But the social functions of monks being admitted, there is not even that in favour of Thelema,—apart, indeed, from the hypothesis that their studies were of the highest social importance[1]. At all points, therefore, when he was planning Thelema, the author appears either to have neglected the claims of religion or to have subordinated it to what was in his mind of far greater weight—the advancement of learning. Later the discovery and examination of the enigma demonstrate this attitude: Gargantua wishes to explain it as an allegorical description of the Reformation, but Friar John, interpreting it as it was meant to be[2], laughed

[1] This hypothesis seems to have been accepted by Dolet, with whom Rabelais was at that time associated. See his Prefaces to the Commentaries on the Latin Tongue, quoted by Christie, Etienne Dolet, the Martyr of the Renaissance.
[2] Tilley, François Rabelais, pp. 160–1.

that whimsical notion out of court and preferred to regard it as meaning a game of tennis. What an opportunity for a sincere reformer! and what type of man could so sport with so earnest a theme! At least the author held dispassionate views on the subject of religion; and we may find ample confirmation of this view in the educational scheme.

The young Gargantua was trained to perform religious exercises with ordinary regularity. He gave thanks for his food, and for the marvels of the universe that he beheld; and in so doing and in entrusting himself to God for the future, he ratified his faith in the Creator[1]. But what shall be said of the author's view of faith which allowed him, in combating his readers' scepticism on the manner of Gargantua's birth, to describe it as being in 'matters not apparent[2]'? Surely the whole point of such ridicule of the Sorbonne lies in the author's personal conviction that the world was easily comprehensible,

[1] *G.* 23: 'Si prioient Dieu le createur en l'adorant, et ratifiant leur foy envers luy, et le glorifiant de sa bonte immense: et luy rendans grace de tout le passe, se recommandoient a sa divine clemence pour tout l'advenir. Ce faict, entroient en leur repos.'

[2] *G.* 6: 'Je me doubte que ne croyez asseurement ceste estrange nativité. Si ne le croyez, je ne men soucie, mais un homme de bien, un homme de bon sens croit tousjours ce quon luy dit, et quil trouve par escrit. Ne dit Salomon...? Et Sainct Paul prim. Corinthior. xiii, *Charitas omnia credit?* Pourquoy ne le croiriez vous? Pour ce, dictes vous, quil ny a nulle apparence. Je vous dis que, pour ceste seule cause, vous le devez croire, en foy parfaicte. Car les sorbonnistes disent que foy est argument des choses de nulle apparence.'

that faith was of no importance, or what is almost the same thing, that reformist faith was different from the orthodox. Is it not fairly clear that, in the later use of the word, 'faith' must connote the conventional profession of faith and not any personal conviction? And what may be judged of the author's feeling for Christianity,—and we have seen that the Bible in the original tongues was an essential part of all education,—when the reading of the Scriptures was compressed into the time of toilet and dressing[1]? We feel the truth of Ponocrates' ideal 'turning every hour of the day to some use' ('Comment Gargantua fut institue en telle discipline quil ne perdoit heure du jour'), and we estimate this exercise quite as much as a lesson in rhetoric as in theology. No doubt, since these were people like those qualified to enter Thelema, they interrupted their toilet activities by 'giving themselves up to revering, worshipping, praying and supplicating God, whose majesty and marvellous judgments were revealed in the passage read.' In this extensive and detailed educational scheme there is less sincere religious feeling than in Gargantua's letter, above mentioned, and even though the characters of *Gargantua* are of a more

[1] 'Apres, en tel train d'estude le mit *quil ne perdoit heure quelconques du jour: ains tout son temps consommoit en lettres et honneste scavoir*. S'esveilloit donc Gargantua environ quatre heures du matin. Ce pendant quon le frottoit, luy estoit leue quelque pagine de la divine Escripture, haultement et clairement, avec prononciation competente a la matiere' (*G.* 23).

elevated sort than those of *Pantagruel*, they betray
little concern with religion. Grandgousier and his son
are mainly different because the former wholly believes in the saints and holy men of God, whom
priests misrepresent, while the latter cannot do so.
Gargantua's apparently Christian policy towards the
conquered may be more truly described as Platonist,
but, in any case, it was dictated by calculations the
basis of which was perhaps unsound. When Grandgousier had conquered Alpharbal, King of Canarre,

instead of treating him miserably, harshly imprisoning him,
and putting him to ransom at unheard of sums,—as other
kings and emperors, even those who call themselves
Catholic, had done,—he treated him courteously and
amiably; he lodged him in his personal quarters; and with
incredible magnanimity he sent him back under safe-
conduct, laden with gifts and favours and all the kindnesses
of friendship. And what came of it? Returned to his land,
he had all the princes and estates of the kingdom assembled;
he expounded to them the humanity he had experienced;
and he begged them to deliberate on it. . . . Then it was
decreed unanimously that they should offer to us their
lands, domains, and the whole kingdom, to do with them
as seemed good to us (G. 50).

On that precedent Gargantua acted, not upon Christian principles[1]. There is as little Christian spirit in
this illusory statesmanship as in Friar John's glory in

[1] Cp. Rabelais' later reproofs of such prudential Christianity.
In Livy 26. 50 Scipio shows somewhat similar clemency to the
conquered.

fighting[1]; and indeed this greatest of Rabelais' creations displayed a paganism entirely out of keeping
with the feeblest religious sentiment. Both the friar
and his creator were apparently quite unmoved thereby, though each paid lip-service to the creed of the
day. Rabelais must have been influenced by the more
positive beliefs of his fellows,—his artistic sensitive-
ness would prove that,—and when he had to adopt
notions of the Deity he took up either the Old
Testament God of battles or the Renaissance conception of Absolute Reason[2]. Before the influence
of Lyons had worked its will on his mind, the former
found favour, afterwards the latter; but always it is
an intellectual and therefore unstable creed that found
expression. God gave the victory in battle to Pantagruel and to Gargantua, and the prosecution of
Rabelais' nature-studies demanded a formal, if per-
functory, belief in the Creator of so wonderfully an
ordered universe.

When we come to the mature portion of his work
we discover that in this respect an important change
of views must have taken place. Human reason became ever less reliable and the irrational in proportion

[1] G. 39. The friar's pugnacity spoils a passage which might
otherwise be compared with Pantagruel's story of the Death of
Pan (Q. L. 28), for while he scorns the cowardice of the
disciples who left Christ to fall into his enemies' hands, he
equally hated the fugitives from the battle of Pavia.
[2] Cp. inter alia, G. 31: 'rien nest sainct ny sacre a ceulx qui
se sont emancipés de Dieu et raison pour suivre leurs affections
perverses.'

a more important phenomenon; and this cannot but
have been the effect of his having lived actively among
men whose actions were no more rational than those
of most human beings, and with whom reasonable
reforms had been seen to be of no weight[1]. What had
been downright assertions became therefore so hesitating that, in accordance with his observations of
human nature, his views are rather *felt* than expressed.
They are vague, unless some topic profoundly stirs
him; but nevertheless they are so certain and so powerfully suggested that the tone of the later books becomes
almost definitely religious. The younger man looked
at religion as external; the older felt it as inward and
personal experience. In the interval he must have
had thoughts, aspirations, and intuitions, such as are
essentially religious.

For this reason he was bound to orient afresh his
attacks on the religious orders and on formal church
systems. The friars became monsters on account of
their absurd, inhuman and hypocritical customs; the
orthodox clergy took the form of idle and vain pos-
turing birds, whose every action was controlled by
the tinkling of bells; and the new sectarians were
pictured as jealously guarding the most ridiculous
superstitions. Most important of all, his new view of
the monks is that they are more afraid of trans-

[1] This may have been the reason why Rabelais conjured up
such grotesque imaginary scenes. They are such as, by horrify-
ing or amusing his readers, would feelingly persuade them to
adopt conclusions where reasonable arguments left them cold.

gressing the rules of their orders than of breaking the laws of God. Among religious people there are the same faults as of old, but the basis of Rabelais' disapproval is broader, and the externalism of their worship is emphasized. There is a subtly conveyed impression that the travellers wholly fail to sympathize with the two main creeds[1]; their fellowship with the old Macrobe (*Q. L.* 25) is indeed far closer. Hippothadée felt, and the reader is made to feel, that he must expound to an unconverted company the most elementary theological truths; and in the course of his attempted persuasion and the keen debate, he was compelled to reduce his beliefs to the conception of a Supreme Creator in whose Bible humanity must seek for all the guidance they need (*T. L.* 30). Therein Panurge will find that his marriage will be happy

if he takes his wife from among honest people, instructed in virtue and honesty, having frequented only pure society, loving and fearing God, delighting in pleasing God in faith and the observance of His holy commandments, fearing to offend Him and lose His favour by transgression of His divine law, and commanded to cherish and wholly serve him after God.

We need not here point out how fully such a comprehensive mass of conditional advice is inappropriate to the context. We may also for the moment neglect Panurge's disbelief in such a woman's ever being found or even discoverable. But we must note that

[1] Cp. *T. L.* 48, where Gargantua denounces the 'pastophores taulpetiers' for interposing between parents and children.

later on when Trouillogan's contradictions compelled the perplexed travellers to consider other
examples, Hippothadée contributed a Biblical text
as if he were puzzled by it, and that Pantagruel
expounded it (*T. L.* 35). The self-confessed interpreter of the Bible had found no real guidance, and
had apparently sought and triumphantly found in
the words of the 'Holy Envoy' what he considered to
be a better instance of ineffectual philosophy than
that cited by Rondibilis; and Pantagruel's inexpert
interpretation shows that the text had no bearing
upon Panurge's problem[1]. Again, unlike Rondibilis
and indeed all the company, Hippothadée naturally
trusts wholly to the story of the Fall of Man. To
him the Bible appears incontrovertibly true and comprehensive of all man's interests for all time, literally
true in spite of his being unable to decipher it; while

---

[1] Speaking of Trouillogan, Gargantua says: 'Je l'entends
en mon advis. La response est semblable a ce que dist un ancien
philosophe interroge s'il avoit quelque femme quon luy nom-
moit. Je lay, dist il, amie; mais elle ne me a mie. Je la possède,
d'elle ne suis possede....' 'Ainsi, dist Rondibilis, mettons nous
neutre en medecine, et *moyen en philosophie, par participation de
l'une et l'aultre extremite....*' 'Le Sainct Envoye, dist Hippo-
thadee, me semble, l'avoir plus apertement declaire (i.e. the
philosophical position?) quand il dit: Ceux qui sont maries soient
comme non maries; ceux qui ont femme soient comme non
ayans femme.' After giving his explanation Pantagruel adds:
'Prenant en ceste maniere avoir et n'avoir femme *je ne voy
repugnance ne contradiction es termes.*' It is a lesson in moderation, he thinks; but it does not, as Hippothadée believes, confirm scholastic philosophy; nor is the truth of the text confirmed
by the futile study.

the travellers seem to have considered that of necessity it was not quite abreast of modern thought and knowledge, and may be too profoundly serious for petty human affairs to be dealt with in it[1]. They seem to have shared Pantagruel's confident hopes for the future and, like him, to have sought in human knowledge legitimate bases for interpreting divine revelations. It is the same process of thought that appears, as we have noted in the last chapter, in Rabelais' view of ancient literature. Was not this probably his personal opinion on the Bible? Pantagruel had refused to be bound by the Law of Moses (Calvin's great source of authority) when it forbade resort to witches; and the dignified reproof that Panurge's sceptical remark drew from Hippothadée was later turned against the theologian's fellow-believers in predestination doctrines[2]. We may be certain that Rabelais was incapable of believing in the letter of

[1] *T. L.* 30. Panurge says: 'Vous voulez donc que j'espouse la femme forte, descrite par Salomon? Elle est morte, sans poinct de faulte. Je ne la vis onque, que je saiche: Dieu me le veuille pardonner,' and again, 'Vous me remettez au conseil prive de Dieu, en la chambre de ses menus plaisirs.'

[2] Cp. Prologue de l'Auteur, *Q. L.*: 'Voire mais, dictes vous, Dieu men eust aussi tost donne soixante et dix huit mille comme la treiziesme partie d'un demy. Car il est tout puissant. Un million d'or luy est aussi peu qu'un obole. Hay, hay, hay. Et de qui estes vous apprins ainsi discourir et parler de la puissance et predestination de Dieu, pauvres gens? Paix st, st, st, humiliez vous davant sa sacree face et recognoissez vos imperfections....Ainsi ne font les Genevois....Ilz ne se contentent de sante, d'abondant ilz souhaitent gaing, voire les escuz de Guadaigne.'

the Bible, which was demanded by Calvin, whether he accepted the spirit or no. Theologians and their flocks were, in Rabelais' eyes, presumptuous in that they claimed to know God's purposes; and that was at bottom the travellers' opinion. Perhaps we may go further and say that Rabelais considered a creed, which did not aim at correcting human behaviour, an idle and mischievous one. He at least could not hope for worldly profit from his religious convictions[1]; and his plans had been too often strangely thwarted for him to believe so simply.

The same line separated the travellers from Homenas to whom they appeared as alien as to Hippothadée, and in whose company they were quite as ill at ease as in that of the *Isle Sonante* birds; and their strange discomfort cannot solely have been owing to his excessive reverence for the papal bulls. It may be quite true that Rabelais took advantage of the popular discontent with paying first-fruits to Rome and of the strong recurrent agitation for an independent Gallican Church, but Homenas, apart from his unpopular opinions, would necessarily have

[1] Note the arguments that he puts into Hippothadée's mouth (*T. L.* 30): 'Quand je vous dis: S'il plaist a Dieu, vous fais je tort? Nest ce honorer le Seigneur, createur, protecteur, servateur? Nest ce le recognoistre unique dateur de tout bien? Nest ce nous declairer tous despendre de sa benignite? Rien sans luy nestre, rien ne valoir, rien ne pouvoir si sa saincte grace nest sus nous infuse? *Nest ce mettre exception canonicque a toutes nos entreprinses* et tout ce que nous proposons remettre a ce que sera dispose par sa saincte volonte?'

to represent a considerable number of moderate Catholics[1]. A general resemblance, which shall throw into relief the exaggerated or fictitious elements, is essential to the effective satire of which Rabelais was then capable; and we rather belittle his artistic powers when we explain such a long episode as resulting from so wide-spread an agitation. The fundamental difference between the host and his guests leaps to the eyes at every moment of their intercourse. By 'Celuy qui est' Homenas means not God, but His 'representative on earth'; indeed the Pope becomes 'this God on earth[2]'; and his highest praise of the blessed decretals is that they draw gold from France. It can hardly be doubted that Homenas' conception of religion was of the external and accidental features of Church government, which had destroyed or dissipated all feelings of mystery; and Pantagruel's conception of 'Celuy qui est' is simple and humble and full of reverence for the mystery of the Godhead. '"He who is,"' he says, 'is God, according to our theological doctrine. And He declared Himself in so

[1] 'Les prescheurs decretalistes' is a Rabelaisian phrase from the time of Gargantua (G. 42): they maintained that 'quiconque verra son prochain en danger de mort, il le doibt, sus peine d'excommunication trisulce, plus tost admonester de soy confesser et mettre en estat de grace que de luy aider.' They are obviously Catholics.

[2] Q. L. 50: 'Que vous semble de ceste image?' 'Cest, respondit Pantagruel, la ressemblance dun pape....' 'Vous dictes bien, dist Homenas. Cest lidee de celluy Dieu de bien en terre, la venue duquel nous attendons devotement, et lequel esperons une fois voir en ce pays.'

many words to Moses. Certainly we never saw Him, nor is He visible to mortal eyes'; and in that mood, Friar John's recollection of a monkish saying and his explanation ('tu as une jambe de Dieu') provoke Pantagruel's indignant outcry at connecting such disgusting anecdotes with true religious feeling[1]. It is doubtful whether these liberal and, in our modern sense of the word, truly religious sentiments could have been accepted either by Calvinists or Catholics[2]. Rabelais' early ideas had been limited to the externals of worship, to ceremonies and formal professions; he seems later to have moved steadily towards mystical views.

Compared with the logical and dogmatic doctrines of 'the demoniacal Calvin of Geneva,' the scene in Raminagrobis' death-chamber contains something infinitely affecting. 'Go, my children,' said the dying poet as he gave his paper of advice into their hands,

Go in the protection of the God of Heaven, and trouble me no more with this or any other matter whatsoever. This very day, which is the last of May and of me ('de May et de moy'), I have expelled from my house with great trouble and difficulty a pack of wretched unclean and pestilential beasts...who would not let me die at ease...and who

[1] Cp. p. 31.
[2] Pantagruel's disagreement with the Calvinists appears even in the visit to Papefiguière, of which the outstanding feature was gross superstition (*Q. L.* 45–7), and with the Catholics when he saw them going to Chesil to redact new laws against heretics (*Q. L.* 18). Guillaume du Bellay seems to have held similar views.

recalled me from the sweet thoughts in which I acquiesced, seeing, contemplating, nay touching and tasting the good and happiness that God has prepared for His faithful and His chosen.... Leave their paths, be not like unto them, trouble me no longer and, I beg you, leave me in silence (*T. L.* 21).

The scenes of death, at which Rabelais had been present, had made a deep impression upon his mind. He believed in an all-powerful God before whom mankind must humble but not prostrate themselves, and in whose actions one can but imperfectly trace the slightest purpose. Time after time he insisted that man must trust that God's purposes are good, and must be resigned to them. Properly and reverently interpreted, the Bible *will* guide man's actions[1]; but he was convinced that man must not rely upon external help alone. 'Man's salvation lies partly in the will of God, partly in his own discretion[2]'; and he was convinced that slothful idleness and fatalism on the part of man irritate God ('Si en necessite et dangier est lhomme necgligent, eviré et paresseux, sans propos il implore les dieux. Ilz sont irrités et indignés'). It is easy to see how Rabelais had arrived

[1] Accounting for a sudden resumption of his romance when discouragement had given him a distaste for it, he wrote: 'Tel est le vouloir du tres bon, tres grand Dieu, onquel je acquiesce, auquel je obtempere, duquel je revere la sacrosaincte parole de bonnes nouvelles, cest l'Évangile, onquel est dict, Luc IV, en horrible sarcasme et sanglante derision..."Medecin, o gueriz toy mesmes"' (Prologue de l'Auteur, *Q. L.*). Note the personal reference of the text to himself.
[2] Cp. footnote in W. F. Smith's Translation on *Q. L.* 23.

at these speculations; easy to detect the difference between his practice and that of his fellows. Rabelais, the old dangerously speculative Rabelais, could not wholly accept current Christian doctrines because experience had taught him that other and older thoughts contained truth. Much of his liberalism was probably an offshoot of that rooted habit which had made him check one ancient authority by another, or by his knowledge of life and his meditations upon it. He seems to have preferred to confirm the truths of his reading in the Scriptures or in pagan works rather than to rely upon either source of authority and adapt the other to it; but the standard by which he judged must have been life itself. Under conditions that allow of no other conduct he behaved, like Pantagruel, with Christian Stoicism (Q. L. 22); and when he read his Plutarch the Death of Pan aroused within him his finest Christian feelings (Q. L. 28). In reading that narrative, he must be dull indeed who cannot feel beneath the surface a poignantly sensitive sympathy with the dying Christ. Perhaps, it is true, the passage is too human and not sufficiently 'divine' to suit orthodox beliefs, but only reverent study of a little recognized aspect of the subject—at least little recognized in that day—could have produced such a masterpiece of writing[1]. After reading that

[1] Possibly by a small oversight, the author intrudes upon his work, testifying *in propria persona* to the effect of the story upon his master. See note, p. 113.

chapter we cannot be surprised that he will not
attempt in a definite statement to profess his faith
in Christ, for he preferred the emotional appeal to
any dogmatic expression of the thought. As suggested
in the Pan legend, he founded his hopes on the inter-
relations of mankind and nature; and his grandest
hopes were probably that through Nature, through
a life in accordance with natural law, each man
might at last attain to a comprehension of the Deity.
Raminagrobis, as we have seen, looked upon death
as a natural passing into the future state, with which
passage the religious orders and even friends could
not be allowed to interfere; and Pantagruel, the ideal
hero whose life should enlarge humanity's vision, he
too, must pass his days, seeking for truth in the world
and in all varieties of human life, according to his
loftiest conception of God whose centre is everywhere
and whose circumference is nowhere[1]. He must therefore necessarily detach himself from human religious
systems in so far as they were contrary to nature and
in so far as externalisms would clog the movements
of his soul. When Bacbuc sent back the travellers

[1] 'Allez, amis, en protection de ceste sphere intellectuelle de
laquelle en tous lieux est le centre et na en lieu aucun circon-
ference, que nous appelons Dieu' (*Quint Livre*, 48). Cp. *T. L.* 13.
In his later work the thought of God always arouses in him feelings
of humanity's imperfections and *vice versa*: cp. Prologue, *T. L.*,
where speaking of Diogenes he says: 'S'il avoit quelques imperfections, aussi avez vous, aussi avons nous. Rien nest, sinon
Dieu, parfaict.' He, like Hermes Trismegistus (whom he
quotes), adopted this definition as being 'most perfect.'

of themselves to work out their salvation, she did
not, as indeed she needed not, add what was superfluous advice to her farewell. We cannot doubt that
Rabelais believed that 'the Kingdom of Heaven is
within you,' since that is the meaning of the interview with the prophetess; but he would have added
that we must seek it in what lies both within and
without the individual.

The experiences of his early years had not allowed
any feeling for the supernatural to flourish in his
fruitful nature, until he had left his monastic life
well behind him, and his ever-receptive mind had
probably failed to grasp at evidence of the mystery
in things. There had been no mystery indeed because
his objective studies and the externalism of monastic
life had excluded all necessity for serious reflection.
Not even Plato's powerful influence over him had
extended to metaphysics; his thoughts were limited
to the external world, whence probably the strange
confusion of formal religiosity and sordid life. With
his leap on to the world's stage, and still more as he
came to know and admire Guillaume du Bellay, all
this changed. Revealed religion and orthodoxy he
seems never thenceforth to have been able to accept,
his belief in the essential goodness of human nature
perhaps precluding the one, and his preoccupation
with Nature and with ethical and social problems
excluding the other. Indeed it appears probable that
his efforts to establish a working basis for natural

philosophy—which is the interest that can be traced most completely through his work from *Pantagruel* to the last chapter of the *Quint Livre*—were largely thrown away because his way of life and still more his patron's death had impelled him constantly towards metaphysical speculations. His thirst for understanding had turned to good account his ever-widening knowledge of man's inner processes, of man's motives and passions, and had led him to enquire what lay behind phenomena. The old mad joy of living and careless adoption of dogmatic religion for his literary purposes became impossible, and his tentative discoveries and hesitant explanations begot in the student an attitude of mind which must be called religious.

7. THE PHILOSOPHY

WE have seen in the last chapter that there is justification for believing that Rabelais' mind had progressively turned from the externals of religion towards truly religious feeling, and that, in fact, except as a wholesome check upon his moral and metaphysical musings, the world about him became of less fundamental importance to him as time went on. It remains for us to attempt to find whether the same development may be traced in the domain of philosophy. For Rabelais was a philosopher. He was not a mere mocker of his fellows. Nor was he always one whose views on life encouraged and urged men to a joyous abandonment to all pleasures. He was, moreover, a philosopher whose school was life, or possibly whose life enabled him to criticize traditional views, and his thoughts were affected no more by his natural buoyant optimism than by the saddest of convictions. Amidst the most boisterous pages our attention is arrested by some sad phrase. It may indeed hardly be doubted that his definition of Pantagruelism[1] hides the bitter, patient smile of a disappointed man. It was the same man who spoke of the climax and end of the comedy approaching (*Q. L.* 27), when he thought of life and death. And surely something of the same disillusionment explains the sobriety in Bacbuc's rhapsody on natural philosophy compared with the

[1] 'Cest certaine gayete desprit conficte en mespris des choses fortuites' (Prologue de l'Auteur, *Q. L.*).

exuberant hopes of the Pantagruelion passage. That is easily comprehended. But if there be a development in Rabelais' views, and if the conclusion be actually of a much later date, it is obvious that other more subtle *differentiae* should be traceable.

The search for Rabelais' philosophy is difficult. His whole romance is so extensive, his wilfully enigmatic utterances so abundant and his appeal to humanity so powerful that there has been always a temptation for his readers to treat Rabelais as Shakespeare and others have been treated. Yet there is hardly the same difficulty to account for the certain failures which come from reading into sundry portions of the romance the most widely divergent systems of philosophy. Unlike Shakespeare, Rabelais probably never succeeded in curbing his personal likes and dislikes; he never wholly succeeded in taking an objective view of his creation. Even the discussions of the *Tiers Livre* are faulty in this, for they each and every one protrude upon us the simple truth which the author would have us grasp. In every part of the romance we never shake off the author's guiding hand, and we may therefore hope to cut through the windings of his labyrinth and so escape into the light of day. The main difficulty is not one of deciding Rabelais' personal relation to his creatures and their utterances, as it is in Shakespeare; it is one of chronology and of probable development. Most human revaluations time and a changed life will explain; and the change that overtook Rabelais was far greater than any of which we have knowledge from Shakespeare's biography—unless the *Sonnets* hide it. Little, however, as the author of the great tragedies can be recognized in the early worker on still earlier plays, an even wider gap separates the *Tiers* and *Quart Livres* from the two early books. Narrative told for its own sake preceded narrative of a different kind in which from time to time we notice an underlying motive; and we cannot doubt that the fruits of his active life must weigh more heavily than those of his semi-cloistered years. Indeed, contrary to the general practice, we might almost exclude the first two books, so opposed to them is the thought of the mature work; and that would be perhaps justifiable, though it would deprive us of glimpses of the true Rabelais beneath his unnatural trappings.

We have seen above that Rabelais appreciated one difference between himself and his fellows. Others are to be found. Thus the age seems to have assumed that only in the philosophies of Greece and Rome could the slightest basis of thought be found; and indeed in many instances the real substance of ancient literature was forgotten in fashionable raptures over language and style. In that early period, too, and up to a comparatively late stage in Rabelais' career, everything written in the Greek tongue received equal attention from students. Every man, it has been doubtfully said, is born a Platonist or an Aristotelian, with a mind subjective or objective, though the records of that age hardly confirm the view. Certainly the realist author of *Pantagruel* glided readily into the transcendental author of *Gargantua*; and neither the one nor the other wrote the attack upon the Ramus-Galland controversy. The fact is that when he trusted the ancient wisdom he assumed impartially the doctrines of all; when, however, his eyes were opened, he saw clearly how unreal his contemporaries' learning was, and how vainly mankind could look for help to ancient philosophy[1]. Rabelais was not unaffected by either Platonism or Aristotelianism. It is beyond doubt that he savagely attacked all who clung helplessly to the latter, and that he ridiculed the languorous worshippers at the former shrine; but this rather proves his reasoned or instinctive hatred of the past than definite disagreement with the ancient systems. He was prepared to accept their teachings in so far as they could be proved. In his study of Nature he preferred to follow Pliny rather than Aristotle, and thence resulted a certain resemblance to the philosopher whom he attacked. In his general thought, however, he more clearly inclined towards Platonism. At one time the *Republic*, at another the *Laws*, attracted him; but at all times the *Dialogues*

[1] Note Gargantua's outburst (*T. L.* 36): 'A ce que je voy, le monde est devenu beau filz depuis ma cognoissance premiere. ...Vrayement on pourra doresnavant prendre les lions par les jubes....Mais ja ne seront telz philosophes par leurs paroles pris.'

centring round Socrates, and specially the *Memorabilia* of Socrates, were what he delighted in recalling. But —and this is important—these books always charmed his mind because, in the same measure as his experience, they gave him a sense of reality. With little world-knowledge he was satisfied with the *Republic*; greater experience pricked that bubble, and he turned to the *Laws*; but always Socrates seems to have satisfied his greatest needs. And one proof of this lies in his constant rejection of the *Symposium* in spite of his certain acquaintance with it. The gross realism of *Pantagruel*, as well as the Platonism of *Gargantua*, affords the clearest demonstration of Rabelais' sincerity. He appears to have been always sensitively responsive to outside influences[1], and until he had laid down a course for himself the predominant creed among his immediate associates would always induce belief in him. It is not therefore surprising that having left in turn his vagabond student's life which gave him his first book, and the cultured society of Lyons (Thelema) to enter the world of statesmen and practical men, who are of necessity least bound by academic views, he should have responded in like manner to worldly influences. His mature work was no more Platonistic than the people among whom he spent his days. In the same way his gross egotism, purified by Platonism, almost loses itself in the humble student

[1] Note his fondness for scenes and incidents connected with himself. See pp. 18–19, 27–8, etc.

of man and the world, of the later books[1]. His choice of a profession had somewhat contributed to this change: it had forced upon him interests which, as we can trace in his writings, corrected his unwholesome passion for self-approving display; but it was his delight in all that seemed real to him that had governed his actions from first to last. We can trace that from book to book, under all its disguises. That is the source of his vitality, of his charm, and of his sordid imaginings. His later moderated self-revelation made of Pantagruel a truly notable character, and commended his work to the most varied types of mind. Surely the man who conceived such a hero, and who combined in him an extensive knowledge of ancient philosophy, introspective insights, and strong interest in the world about him,—surely such a man cannot truly be styled a follower of Aristotle or of Plato. He united the best elements of his race with the most vital energy of Renaissance learning, and he left the past on a voyage of discovery.

The tumultuous movement of the later books, instinct with life and development, clearly demon-

[1] Thus his early dreams of freedom ('Fais ce que vouldras') challenge comparison with the fable of the horse and the ass, told by Panurge (*I. S.* p. 17). The ass says: 'Aussi nest-ce mon estat suyvre les courts des grands seigneurs, nature ne ma produit que pour l'ayde des pauvres gens. Esope me en avoit bien adverti par un sien apologue.' We are not free to choose freedom or servitude, a much more positive opinion than is to be found in the inconclusive discussion (*T. L.* 7) on how far individual whims may be permitted.

strates a more satisfactory freedom than the much
boasted dream of Thelema. Without demanding conformity with a preconceived ideal, mankind shall
henceforth pursue truth, and find freedom in their
search. Not selfish gratification but freedom of the
mind to seek and ensure real human welfare became
his later ideal. He himself made the journey to the
source of truth, and mankind must do likewise.
Characteristically his search began with an actual
problem, or rather with several urgent questions of
the day. Characteristically too, in his enquiries into
marriage and prognostication, he ransacked learning
and commonplace stories; and he mingled with his
spoils his personal convictions and the results of
personal observation. Truth, he would seem to say,
must be human truth; it is of no advantage to raise
questions of the Absolute. Our truths must be of the
earth and must shed light upon practical matters, and
so philosophers and theologians could not be of much
service. And if the avowed purpose of the *Tiers Livre*
—the discussion of Panurge's marriage—became
almost hopelessly confused, it was because in his
quest other equally pressing problems rose in his mind
and overflowed into his writing. The one positive
subject had led him on to revise all his former values.
To compress into such a book all that he had considered, Rabelais would have needed, nay he had
probably discovered in the process of composing it
that he needed, all the moderation that he later urged

upon his readers. For beside the two main topics, there is much in the repeated statement that decision and will-power must be cultivated. Not only Panurge, but the author and human kind also must be trained to decide and act decisively, putting aside the delusive fancy that they may forecast the future. And then too there is the question of death and human destiny, which for the first time rose in the author's written thoughts, but which became more and more insistent. On that question he appears already to have taken up the stand of his maturity in that he combined a sense of mystery with a passionate love of earth, 'lalme et grande mere la terre' (*T. L.* 48). To what he could be sure of he clung with pathetic violence, to earth and worldly interests; and almost with horror he began to reject Platonist abstractions.

He was convinced that only a comprehensive study of human nature could quiet doubts on the marriage institution and could reveal the truth about it; he asserted time and again that human needs alone[1] may adequately explain human inventions. For him no other conceivable explanation existed, and Panta-gruelism could do no more than carry further what physical need (Messer Gaster) had already originated. He revered that mythical being in consequence, but he became enthusiastic over humanity's future triumphs. And in spite of Rabelais' supposed delight

[1] Cp. Prol. de l'Auteur, *Q. L.*: 'Comme vous scavez que necessite fut inventrice d'eloquence.'

in the things of the body, the physical really occupied
no more than a subordinate place in his thoughts.
'Nevertheless,' he wrote, 'Gaster confessed that he
was a poor, common and wretched creature, and not
a god' ('Ce nonobstant Gaster confessoit estre non
dieu, mais pauvre vile chetifve creature'—*Q. L.* 60).
He was but a means to man's development. He was
not the central truth of existence, but if men would
progress at all towards their destined greatness, they
must not neglect the means by which they had
already advanced. Their great physical needs will
lead them to explore 'the springs of hail, the bounds
of rain and the workshops of thunderbolts' (*T. L.* 51)
since such inexplicable phenomena threaten their
existence, while if they neglect realities they may
become as ineffectual as the lady of Entelechie who
dominates her 'affections.' It is true that humanity
has nobler means of advancement than Gaster had,
but the most notable discoveries will be those which
satisfy positive necessities. On the other hand, man
must avoid the error of the Gastrolatres (Pantagruel
denounces them (*Q. L.* 58)), who had conceived a new
god Ventripotent, apparently when Gaster declined
divine honours; who had erected a statue, Manduce[1],

---

[1] Here again Rabelais had apparently been inspired from
actual life. Speaking of Manduce, he says: 'A Lyon, au car-
naval, on l'appelle Maschecroutte; ils la nommoient Manduce.
Cestoit une effigie monstrueuse, ridicule, hideuse, et terrible
aux petits enfants,' etc. (*Q. L.* 59). Note his later tenderness for
little children.

to his glory; who had ordained manifold sacrifices
to him; and who had in short fallen to worshipping
their basest corporeal desires. Their peculiar sin,
in Pantagruel's (Rabelais') eyes, was that they
had wholly distorted an important truth: they had,
reversing Calvin's words, transformed a philosophy
into a religion[1]. In all things moderation must have
its place (Prol. de l'Auteur, *Q. L.*); it is praised
under all circumstances (*T. L.* 13); it is even praised
by Panurge, when occasion demands (*Q. L.* 7).
Moderation, however, insists that mankind shall not
neglect the physical in favour of the intellectual, or
vice versa; and one result of the extreme reaction
from gross debauchery was an even greater danger
of plunging into spiritual or intellectual excess[2]. This
is the thought that underlies his praise of Physie and
scorn of Antiphysie (*Q. L.* 32), in which the former
is the blending of all the elements of human nature,
while the race of the other comprises individuals who
suffer from some excess. The existence of Antiphysie
and her brood demanded some explanation, and the
secret was her excessive maternal fondness. In spite
of the obvious deformities of her monstrous children,
she had so frequently maintained that they were

[1] See p. 7, n. 1.
[2] Entelechie in the *Quint Livre* is surely his clearest exposition of his moderate views. The close resemblance between
Rabelais' mature views and the Nicomachean Ethics, of which
he was aware (*G.* 10), but which till this time he had not
adopted, can hardly be accidental. Life had convinced him
of the truth of those teachings.

'more beautiful and attractive than Physie's off-
spring' that 'by the testimony of brute beasts, she
drew all the fools and mad folk to her opinion, and
she was held in admiration by all witless folk and by
those who were deprived of good judgment and common sense[1].' Only by such men could the mother of
Beauty and Harmony be neglected. In man what is
natural must include the animal and the spiritual, and
to interpret natural as brutal or stupid was apparently the error of 'fools and mad folk,' who are
likely to run to extremes. They are like the good
Bishop Tinteville of Auxerre who, having noted that
hailstorms destroyed his vines on certain saints' days,
had those festivals transferred to mid-winter so that
the saints could do him no further harm (*T. L. 33*).
They are like Homenas and Panurge who seek to
fashion systems of philosophy on preconceived notions;
and they, if any, are likely to consider that enquiries
into marriage should not turn upon the facts of man
and woman's place in nature, but rather upon transcendental conceptions. They may hold that Rondibilis'
method was insulting to woman, but if so they could
not—as Rondibilis did, insisting upon the certainties
of life—convert the question into whether it be
possible that reason and common sense could ultimately subjugate and control animal nature and

[1] The parabolic demonstration bespeaks a mind of which
the natural tendency would be towards expression in meta-
phors, cp. p. 33.

animal desires. Transcendentalists offered no practical help; the physician could point to 'certain worthy women' who had in fact solved the great problem. Naturally, since his philosophy is founded upon a Renaissance student's perceptions of facts, it represents the triumphs of common sense[1], in itself proof of a remarkable superiority to the philosopher's contemporaries.

However there is much more than common sense in the later thought. Interest in reality and consequently some neglect of supramundane matters had given him dreams of a system of natural philosophy. And although his work marked little positive advance because, despite his closest scrutiny of ancient scientific lore, he always demanded scientific learning from the Ancients, he compared most satisfactorily in point of achievement with his contemporaries and many of his immediate successors, who claimed to be men of science, and who were actually more favourably placed for scientific study[2]. He was more independent than they of Hearsay ('Ouy-dire'); and even his strong faith in Nature did not run to such extremes as that of lesser men. To him the natural world seemed far from perfect[3], yet it is that of which man

[1] A critical opinion, equally applicable to the literary revolution of 1660. See M. Faguet's *Propos Littéraires*, Series 2.

[2] Petit de Julleville, *Histoire de la littérature*, etc. vol. III, p. 14; also M. Sainéan's articles (*R. S. S.* 1915) referred to above.

[3] 'Vray est comme en toutes choses Dieu excepte advient quelquefois erreur. Nature mesmes nen est exempte quand elle produict choses monstrueuses et animaux difformes' (*I.S.*p. 22).

can obtain the most certain knowledge. Indeed Pantagruelion had inspired him with enthusiasm for possible progress; it had appeared to him to be the only means whereby mankind might be newly tempered for its search for truth, and through which the new spirit, undaunted by burnings and persecutions, should cause the old gods to tremble at mankind's power. The vision of man scaling heaven and spreading dismay among 'celestial minds' ('intelligences celestes') provokes comparison with Bacbuc's exhortation to the returning pilgrims; but the visionary's study of nature had, long before the arrival at the Oracle, considerably moderated his enthusiasm. No longer did he hope for superhuman powers from scientific knowledge, but all that he dreamed of was to ameliorate mankind's lot on earth. In the later account there is disillusionment and disappointment. His task had proved not so simple as he had believed, but it had become more definite and less fantastic.

'What has become of the art among you which wise Prometheus discovered?' cried Bacbuc. 'What has become of the art of calling down from heaven thunderbolts and celestial fire? Of a truth you have lost it. It has left your hemisphere, but here underground it is in use. And you are wrong in being sometimes aghast when you see towns burning through thunderbolts and lightning, and in being ignorant of whence, by whom and from whom this fearful horror comes upon you. To us it is useful and quite ordinary' (*Quint Livre*, 48).

We have seen on a former page that Rabelais de-

liberately attempted to defeat the powers of superstition, and he seems to have concluded that, until
mankind was liberated from their dreads, no progress
was possible. But, although with his old zeal he still
maintained that all possible recesses of knowledge
should be explored[1], he manifestly felt that the main
stumbling block—as it was the strongest support of
superstition—was the servile worship of antiquity.
True he did not present in its proper relation with
this theme the suggestion, made elsewhere, that this
reverence for authority sprang from a desire for quiet
in an unresting world; nor did he, as elsewhere, pro-
claim the limitations of the human intellect. Those
facts would perhaps have injured the intended effect
of this passage. But he did assert that a new spirit,
which should not let men shrink from the unknown
as Panurge did from the Frozen Words, must come
upon mankind; and in addition to the material progress with which (in the *Tiers Livre*) he had been
concerned, he did propose to make intellectual and
moral progress. In short Rabelais' life had taught him
that scientific and moral advance must be one, and
that consequently neither he nor his fellows could
hope to realize their high ambitions. The travellers
in search of truth must return, not empty-handed,
but possessed of the certainty that truth is relative
to the hearts and minds of the searchers.

Yet this moral emphasis was no new element in

[1] Cp. Voulté's opinion of Rabelais, p. 10.

Rabelais' thought. The Olympians say to one another that

Pantagruel will marry; and he will have children by whom a herb will be discovered that shall conduct them to the springs of hail, the channels of rain and the workshop of thunder. They will invade the regions of the moon and, entering the territory of the constellations, they will be able to sit at table with us and take to wife our goddesses, which is the only way to be deified (*T. L.* 51).

Now this final reference to the marriage question was necessary only in so far as it may connect the vision of progress with the discussions of a practical problem. No doubt in the *Tiers Livre* some mention of marriage was to be expected even in the Pantagruelion section; but the peculiar phrasing would suggest that Rabelais was convinced that human problems depend for their solution upon a wider knowledge of Nature, or even that those problems were the chief reason for his scientific curiosity. In the absence of the deeper comprehension of existence there may be certain phenomena to trouble man's basal principles, those principles across and upon which his existence is laid; and the enthusiastic student of science realized that until a moral reformation came to pass those phenomena could not even be analyzed. Rabelais was, it seems, more deeply interested in man than in pure scientific knowledge, hence, no doubt, his reliance upon ancient writers in this respect; and by urging his fellows to press onwards to a full knowledge of Nature's most mysterious retreats, he tried to confine the supernatural and the incomprehensible to a much smaller area. To that task, the real work of the future[1], he had been permitted to set his hand. And though he had obtained only a hazy view of the promised land, Bacbuc's vision, thus interpreted, would become a worthy conclusion to his whole work. Not purely scientific, that passage would in fact represent the purpose about which he was wholly in earnest.

To dwell too much upon his supposed system of natural philosophy would necessitate the neglect of the more important incidental discoveries that he had made. Certainly the discoverer more dearly prized the insights into life and human nature than his fairly obvious plan which they threw into confusion[2]. From the beginning his main attention had been engrossed by the lives of his fellows, and though his learning and the fulfilment of immediate purposes had obscured this characteristic yet, as we have

[1] Both in the Pantagruelion chapters and in Bacbuc's speech the feeling that, after all, future ages must accomplish the work he suggested is very strong.

[2] If we suppose that the conclusion of the *Quint Livre* was— even in outline—planned at the time of the prospective voyage, the intense interest in various episodes which are superior to that conclusion must show that Rabelais prized those later discoveries. If the last chapters of the *Quint Livre* were of a later date, the fact that the author did not see them through the press would help to explain the feeling of disappointment that the reader must have after so many more excellent episodes. In view of the matter of the two portions a re-handling of a previous sketch would appear reasonable, and any unsatisfactory vagueness would then be the effect of abstraction.

seen[1], this living interest pierced repeatedly through the deadening covering. Apparently nothing had been too trivial to arouse his inquisitive nature; and it is therefore an important sign that his love for Plutarch survived and even became more fervid in after life, in spite of much material that he could not help disputing. In Plutarch first the interest in living beings and then the strong ethical interest gripped him; and his reading fostered in him a taste for depicting the manifold strange peoples, each of which represents some moral distinction. From the beginning also mankind's obsession with the question whether they might foretell events had fascinated him. At first, no doubt, the subject had made him scornfully angry or contemptuous[2]; it was unworthy of an enlightened age. Later, however, he had seriously weighed the evidence and had rejected most of it as false; indeed, it may be half in mockery he had assumed the seer's rôle himself[3]. Nevertheless, in spite of his reasoned rejection of dreams and other divinatory methods, he seems to have retained a secret feeling that, though undemonstrable, forecasting events may be possible; perhaps indeed the process of mocking prophets and their prophecies in the *Tiers Livre* vision had in part

[1] P. 46.

[2] Apart from the *Pantagrueline Prognostications*, he wrote in a letter to the Bishop of Maillezais on prophecies: 'De ma part je ny adjouste foy aucune.'

[3] This seems to have been the first idea of the Pantagruelion chapters, but as he went on the subject carried him away.

converted the sceptic. Perhaps he had felt that in so outlining mankind's future he was actually prophesying; but certainly Guillaume du Bellay's conversation just before his death, in which he foretold things 'part of which we have seen come to pass and part we expect to do so,' however naïve it may seem, had troubled his mind and forced him to admit that there were 'more things in heaven and earth than were dreamt of in his philosophy.' He treasured up the words of dying men, for they were more human than a witch's or a conjuror's gesticulations, and so more reliable. Before he had made a real advance in story-telling he had needed a personal interest in the story; and before he could make a real advance in knowledge and thought he needed a personal mystery, an inference that we are justified in making by the only instances in the *Tiers Livre* which show him yielding to a belief rejected by him[1]. Yet the circumstances of that death scene, at which he was present, and which prompted his visit to the Macreons, must have been in keeping with previous examples of his patron's foresight; and surely in their intimacy he must have noted those too. What made the difference was that not only respect for his patron's greatness, but more probably and to a greater extent his consciousness of 'prophetic power' and his passionate human feeling had overcome and pushed aside his pronounced dislike for the mysterious. The

[1] *T. L.* 21.

mystery of the supernatural, in which he still refused
to believe, had paled beside the more profound
mystery of the natural and the human. And in
pondering on these questions he could not help dis-
covering much about human character.

He taught that it is essential that the whole power
of the will should be brought into play; that having
got an assured knowledge of what he desires, every
man must be undeterred by fears or doubts even
though the outcome of his actions may be at variance
with his expectations. Instead of the early thought
through which he beheld the world, and which speaks
of an ordained rise and fall in earthly affairs ('ainsi
ont toutes choses leur fin et periode'—*G.* 31)[1],
Rabelais will fix on the temple walls the better text
which, being an inference from life in the world,
recognizes at least that we may exert will-power to
some effect ('Toutes choses se meuvent a leur fin'—
Quint Livre, 37)[2]. Even in matters of life and death,
as we have seen (p. 155, note 2), he seems to have

[1] A common theme in the early books. In *G.* 31 Gallet
says to Picrochole: 'Si ta maison *debvoit* ruiner, falloit il quen
sa ruine elle tombast sus les atres de celuy qui lavoit aornee?'
Cp. *P.* p. 24: 'Toutes choses seront reduytes a leur fin et periode.'
[2] Rabelais' use of his original in the *Hypnerotomachia* is
instructive. On a tablet was inscribed, according to this book,
on one side *Trahit sua quemque voluntas*, on the other πᾶν δεῖ
ποιεῖν κατὰ τὴν αὐτοῦ φύσιν; for the first of which Rabelais
substituted *Ducunt volentem fata, nolentem trahunt* and for the
second the motto quoted in the text. In both cases Rabelais
stresses the will and the environment with which the will must
strive. He does not apparently believe that the struggle will
be an easy one unless the individual's purposes are in agreement
with the natural trend of things.

considered that man's personality is neither wholly
the sport of the gods, nor wholly a free agent; and
often by merely waiting and persisting he may turn
his experiences to use ('Tout vient a poinct qui peult
attendre'—*Q. L.* 48)[1]. In every part of the later
story, then, Rabelais reiterates the advice which every
man consulted gave to Panurge, and which finally
Bacbuc's words and actions implied. Since the imagination converts simple water into delicious wine, and
since various men will identify the same water as
various kinds of wine, it is obvious that human judgments will be uncertain; and the effect of calculated
rational action being at the best uncertain, it may be
far better to trust to the irrational will[2]. On how far
man's reasoning is valid Rabelais had developed serious
doubts (*T. L.* 44); and he disputed the Peripatetics'
assertion that 'all problems, all questions and all
doubts proposed must be certain, clear and resolvable
by the intelligence' ('tous problemes, toutes questions,
tous doubtes proposés doivent estre certains, clairs,
et intelligibles'—*Q. L.* 63)[3], although he chose to

[1] Though in the context Rabelais was humorously referring
to his visit to the Pope, this should prove that his reflection is the
more serious. See pp. 34–5.

[2] Superficially considered, it may seem to be the teaching of
Thelema. In the early work, however, Reason easily dominated
the will and was synonymous with it. Panurge was incapable
of Reason, only of reasons.

[3] From *G.* 20 and elsewhere we must conclude that in his
early years Rabelais would not have disputed this statement.
In the satire on the Sorbonne, Bragmardo is made to say:
'Raison! nous nen usons poinct ceans.'

give it a curious twist. At the present day we cannot believe that all questions admit of a rational solution: many are only emotionally real and are solved only by 'feeling'; but in the sixteenth century it was a strange doctrine even when Montaigne expounded it. Nor do Rabelais' further remarks invalidate the philosophic conclusion. When Pantagruel ordered dinner in order to set his fellows' insipid doubts to rest he was but reverting to a physiological fact that they had known for a long time[1]; but though, superficially considered, the prince appears to have ridiculed these notions, he certainly thought of the non-intellectual power by which he himself made most of his decisions. At times, he says (*Q. L.* 66), intuitions urged him forward, and at others they restrained him from action; and doubtless this irrational element in his nature controlled his thoughts. There was no other apparent reason than this 'feeling' why he should not land on the Isle of Ganabin (Robbers); and, it must be noted, the inhibition did not affect Friar John, who was the least introspective of the party. 'Go ashore,' he cried, 'go ashore. We shall not have to pay for our quarters. We'll rob and pillage them all.' Apparently Xenomanes was prepared to go ashore. To him the island was an interesting sight, such perhaps as the young Gargantua had sought out

[1] Cp. *T. L.* 13. The debates in *Q. L.* 63 are also 'fades, jejunes, et de maulvaise salive comme estoient leurs corps.'

as part of his education[1], and such as was yet to take
the company into grave danger. The sole reason for
Pantagruel's decision was that he was instinctly re-
pelled, and he, unlike Panurge, could act according
to his resolutions.

Indeed, as from what has been said we might
expect, the central facts of Rabelais' philosophy are
traceable in the contrast between Panurge and his
leader. The former, dreaming of a static world of
selfish delight, unable apparently to profit by his
experiences and his reading, is completely opposed
to the unresting inquisitive spirit and the benevolence
and humanity of Pantagruel; but still more are they
contrasted on all occasions when resolution becomes
necessary[2]. They are united by common human
feelings; they are separated by the gulf between the
noblest progressive character and the commonplace
retrospective being, between the future and the past,
between the possible and the actual. It is indeed
difficult to express the difference between them
because in each of them the personality must be
seen in action to be understood. Each of them lives
by his deeds. Yet surely Panurge's beliefs about
the universe were generally accepted not only by
medieval Christianity, but for the most part by

[1] Cp. the mountebanks, etc. p. 75.
[2] The contrast here is not however that of the early books in
which two intellectual conceptions were embodied, see pp. 45–6.
Between the later Panurge and Pantagruel there is a natural
antipathy.

ancient paganism. They were merely a crude form
of that old-world spirit which sought the Absolute
in everything. And Pantagruel's noble nature proves
that Rabelais denied that spirit. Relative truth is all
that mankind can hope for, and man must be himself
the interpreter of observed facts ('Soyez vous mesmes
interpretes de vostre entreprinse,' said Bacbuc). Not
even man's surest interests stand firm from one period
of his life to another: the author's own life must have
taught him that, and, therefore, the necessity for
adopting Pantagruel's attitude. Rabelais, we feel
assured, saw life and movement in every part, and
specially in man himself; and if, to judge by the above
conclusion, his romance appears to be an extraordinary hoax, it can only be so on the most improbable supposition that at a certain time he had
planned the whole sequel. Bacbuc's vision at the end
of the *Quint Livre* certainly seems to be a memory
of the last chapters of the *Tiers Livre*; but while the
resemblance is slight, the differences alone would
tend to prove that in the meantime Rabelais' views
had changed, and that he had abandoned even the
disruptive interests of science for the less definite but
more fundamental questions of behaviour. Possibly
just as he had remodelled Pantagruel's settlement of
his conquered territory (p. 70) he had set himself to
modify his former vision. We cannot tell, but in spite
of his last book being a posthumous publication there
is enough evidence in Bacbuc's speech to confirm the

teaching of the two central books. The action in them turns upon the idea that a selfish dreamer, whose environment must be arranged so as to satisfy his every desire, will inevitably feel dissatisfaction and discomfort when he has to act on his own initiative in the everyday world. That was one of the prime discoveries which accounted for Rabelais' transformation, for at the beginning of the *Tiers Livre* Panurge and Pantagruel were contrasted in respect of it.

According to the later writings, although most men are unaware of their powers and true purposes, the individual combines legitimate personal rights and duties as a social being whose impulses society's demands must restrain or crush. The conflict between individual liberty and social duty was fought out in Panurge; and it is one of Rabelais' claims to distinction that he offered us no cut-and-dried solution of an age-old problem. His lack of system and his vague views are what we should expect of a sincere man. The difficulty he had grasped, but, perhaps because he realized more and more the vastness of the province that he had undertaken and his own insufficiency, he honestly refrained from adopting one or other of the various philosophies which would have included those broad expanses that he had not explored. His conviction that mankind was not governed by reason, though of slow growth, was constantly strengthened by his observation and supported by his growing personal sympathy with inward religion. He held back from theorizing on man's social relations; he refused to discuss man's relation to God. But whereas, in the early Education Scheme, it had seemed to him reasonable to regard mankind as God's vassals who must pay tribute and service to Him, Rabelais' latest beliefs were that, in aiming at human development, each individual may and must be doing the will of God[1]. In this as in all other respects, even in his dreams of scientific progress, he had left definite views behind him. Like his fellows of all time, he had fashioned his idea of the Creator according to his conceptions of humanity; and his sense of the inexplicable in human nature led him to imagine a non-personal deity, a vague living force, 'whose centre is everywhere and whose circumference nowhere[2].'

[1] Cp. Epistemon's quotation from Sallust (*Q. L.* 23): 'Laide des dieux nest impetree par veuz ocieux, par lamentations muliebres. En veillant, travaillant, soy evertuant, toutes choses succedent a souhait et bon port.'

[2] As nearly always, Rabelais borrows the thought (cp. *T. L.* 13) which suited his conceptions, but his mature idea of God must reflect his idea of man. Rabelais uses the definition twice, but in the second he adopts it as his own. Cp. *Quint Livre*, 48: 'que nous appelons Dieu.'

8. CONCLUSION

ONE further task remains. We must ask what is
Rabelais' place in French literature.

La Bruyère, whose opinion is of the highest importance, higher than Montaigne's somewhat am-
biguous comment, on the whole seems to have
admired the romance, though he regretted its coarseness; and he noted that, in interest and in fundamental
ideas, both Marot and Rabelais were much more
nearly related to the men of letters of the seventeenth
century than the writers of the later sixteenth century
were. So remarkable an inversion of what might be
expected merits attention. With reference to the gulf
that separates the medieval from the modern, our
analysis has again and again revealed the fact that,
if Rabelais' work must be placed, it must be on the
modern side. No matter the subject of which he
treats, his final and mature opinion, if not formed
independently of classical thought, betrays a singularly
free treatment of his masters. Along with men like
Dolet and Marot, he had attempted to turn the new
learning to profit by throwing its light upon current
problems. Rabelais especially had not been content
to study the Ancients for the study's sake. After his
first enthusiasm for literature had sufficiently abated
for him to concentrate his attention upon medicine,
and it may be when he was in frequent contact with
Dolet, he had sought to discover the truths that lay
embedded in much that was worthless in his masters'

works. And as we have seen, he did so in order to solve a purely modern question[1]. In so doing he had acquired the critical outlook upon life and literature which had distinguished the greatest of ancient minds; and having thus plunged deeply into the study of ethical problems, he must have slowly established general principles applicable to all and by which the individual may be judged[2]. In short, in the hands of this Renaissance worker as in those of La Bruyère, La Fontaine, Boileau and Molière, the study of the Ancients had given new life to a modern tongue by transfusing the spirit of ancient literature into essentially modern forms. Like the bees in Swift's *Battle of the Books*, he had extracted the sweetness of that literature, while the spiders fed on the dead matter. He himself appreciated his own tendency in contrast with that of men of his own day[3], particularly 'people who live their lives backwards' and 'certain botchers of old Latin ironwork' (Prol. *T. L.*).

Circumstances had favoured his development. Revolt in the Church and political difficulties gave to students a certain measure of liberty. When, however, the guardians of orthodox beliefs began to

---

[1] Whether it be marriage, or divination, or classical authority in the *T. L.* it was a purely modern question.

[2] The transformation of his satire from savage and blind denunciation to comparatively genial ridicule of vices postulates the development of general principles of conduct. See p. 42.

[3] In Bacbuc's speech he blames the men of his age for losing the art of Prometheus. See p. 172.

associate heterodoxy with the slightest touch of modernism, and when Francis I began to set a course towards repressive despotism, students naturally ceased to criticize life, government or belief and most relapsed into the less dangerous imitation of classical models. This was fatal to literature since it no longer drew its nourishment from the nation's active life; and the literature of the later half of the century, pleasing the court circles, rapidly degenerated. In so far as the Pléiade and the translators, nay even later writers, sought to imitate the Ancients and to conform to their literary principles, they made a retrograde step. For certainly, provided we recognize the importance of the critical period which separates Rabelais' immature work from his mature, the analysis of his thought proves that his relationship to the seventeenth century writers was far more real than that of his immediate successors. Certain elements apart, his views on life were strictly in agreement with, and would cause no surprise if we found them in, the work of that important age.

We have noticed above his free treatment of his originals and his delight in criticizing the faults of his age. Yet surely there is much in the romance which, appropriate to that age, remains true for all time: the stripping of insincerity and the refusal to accept mere appearance bring him very close to Molière. So too does his power of depicting monstrous vicious beings merely by their utterances[1]; but most of all his most cherished view of Nature (Physie) is surely that of his great admirer. The simple natural beings of Molière's plays are the lineal descendants of Physie, and with that ideal before them the two writers could avoid idle and ineffectual savage denunciation. Only when attacking the insincere and the intentionally unnatural were they both provoked to fury. Again Rabelais was endowed with that peculiarly French malice which finds expression at times in Molière and frequently in La Fontaine; and neither of the later writers was more determined in his realism. Nor did La Fontaine more piercingly use the same parabolic power for ridiculing those who abused their social position, even while not caring to offend supporters of the State as it existed. In one sense, apart from his coarseness, and perhaps in only one[2] did Rabelais fall seriously short of the seventeenth century ideal; and yet this defect was and is probably his greatest charm. He lacked the artistic control which those of the later age admirably practised; and only in part can this be explained by the unsettled conditions under which he worked, and which made it a hard task even to compose with the minimum critical attention to his writing. What is more probable

[1] Principally in the posthumous *Quint Livre*, it is true, but Grippeminauld may be well compared with Tartuffe in the influence his presence has over the reader.

[2] Naturally in a more refined period we should not find Rabelais' medieval frankness and coarseness.

is that constantly, and as though he did not care to do otherwise, he gave a very loose rein to his imagination.

We need but recall some of his possible and impossible creations, Messer Gaster, Quaresmeprenant, Grippeminauld and the birds of the *Isle Sonante*; and it must be admitted that on convivial occasions, when he seems to have discovered his narrative powers[1], that power of realizing the most extravagant notions and of ingeniously giving form to abstractions must have greatly helped to divert the company[2]. It must have found escape in the most fascinating anecdotes; no doubt too in speculations which soured persons could look upon as madness, and by which sensitive and earnest souls could be seriously distressed. And certainly his wonderful store of proverbs gave him in abundance material with which to display this peculiarly convivial humour. In actual life he had found that his gross talk, mingled with the joys of feasting and his intellectual brilliance, delighted his hearers; and in his (very successful) *Pantagruel* he attempted to repeat his social successes. In cold print, without the convivial warmth, we feel disappointed with the result. Probably, except in its astounding success, he himself was far from satisfied, for he never at-

[1] Note the zest in *Propos des Beuveurs* and in the feast after Gargantua's victory.
[2] Panurge's adventures at Turkish hands are an early example of Rabelais' clothing extravagant ideas in a realistic dress. *P*. pp. 44–9.

tempted to repeat the experiment. He found little difficulty, however, in slipping from the literal into the metaphorical[1] and in transforming Pantagruelizing from 'eating and drinking as much as you please'; for the transformation he could plead precedents. And thereby he enjoyed and discovered a further intellectual satisfaction, in that he could revel in the whimsically ingenious flights of imagination which, at table, had redeemed his grossness. He could develop the discursive style with which his later work abounds[2]. He could compose those puzzling episodes which throw over his work a false covering of seeming nonsense; and when he wished to write to a purpose this power was most valuable. In those passages he may seem to aim at diverting his readers. Probably this was not so. Having habitually 'set his quill to the wind,' he could not prevent the gale carrying him away; and so powerful was the wind that it often carried him far out of his course. Then, having allowed his genius to thwart his purpose, he had frequently to add in a short perplexing inconsequent passage a brief indication of what he really meant[3].

[1] Thus in *Q. L.* 57 he refers to the earth trembling when Gaster speaks: 'Je vous certifie qu'au mandement de messere Gaster tout le ciel tremble, toute la terre bransle. Son mandement est nommé: faire le fault sans delay, ou mourir.' We may see the old *bon-vivant* making merry over his cups.

[2] The Prologue, *T. L.* is a remarkable example of discursiveness; cp. among others, *T. L.* 45 and Ancien Prologue, *Q. L.*

[3] Cp. *Q. L.* 37-8.

Under such circumstances to obviate misunderstanding he would have needed an astonishing power of self-restraint, or a more polished public; but he was not the man to deny himself the subtle pleasure that discursive writing gives, and in any case he may have scorned the ultra-refinement—which might have made him run great risks. 'To everyone it is not granted to enter and inhabit Corinth,' he says, and he wished to be of service to his fellows; so 'if they wish it and if the wine pleases the taste of the lordship of their lordships, let them drink freely and boldly without payment or stint' (Prologue, *T. L.*). Let him write never so obscurely, 'those who had ears to hear, would hear'; and if they were good Pantagruelists, they would 'never take in bad part whatever things they knew came of a good, frank and loyal heart[1].' To credit him with a fine command of a necessarily inadequate medium is not enough, and yet it may be too much: it may be decidedly misleading. What he certainly lacked was the will and possibly the power to control his luxuriant imagination; and it can hardly be doubted that the superabundance of actions and ideas in his work, coupled with this strange irregularity, would prove the main stumbling-block to La Bruyère's age.

[1] 'Laquelle nos majeurs nommoient Pantagruelisme moyennant laquelle jamais en mauvaise partie ne prendront choses quelconques ilz cognoistront sourdre de bon, franc et loyal coraige' (Prologue, *T. L.*).

INDEX

Amy, Pierre, friend of Rabelais, 2

Andouilles, effect produced by episode upon reader, 36; religious significance, 130–1

Automatism, 38 ff.; *Trouillogan,* 39; *Homenas,* 40

Bacbuc, attitude to Ancients, 117, 182; definition of God, 157

Boyssonné and Voulté, 8; poems on Rabelais' son, 84

Bridoye, 38, 88

Bringuenarilles, 36

Calvin and Rabelais, 6; and knowledge, 20; and belief in Evil, 125–6

Catholic doctrine of that period, 123–4

Characterization: character contrast, 45–7; modified by Platonism, 98–9

Chats Fourrés, 88

Chiquanous, 34, 88

Cop's speech, effect, 7

'*Cymbalum Mundi,*' 6

'*De Inventoribus Rerum,*' 96

Desperiers, 6

Dindenault, Panurge preaches moderation to, 57

Dolet, Etienne: and Rabelais, 1; dinner in honour of his pardon, 4; death, 13;

opinion on the value of learning, 143 *n.*; ideals, 185

Du Bellay, Jean, Cardinal, 3

Du Bellay, Guillaume, Seigneur de Langey: influence on Rabelais, 18, 73; portrayed in '*Pantagruel,*' 66–7; effect of death on Rabelais, 133

Editus describes the entrants to religious institutions, 77; laments his unhappy life, 78

Education schemes, 74–6

Ennasin, 33; social significance, 85; satire of Platonism, 108

Entelechie: employments of officers, 33; lady of *E.'s* reception of travellers, 42; comparison with *Niphleseth* and the 'haulte dame,' 83

Epistemon, 20; denounces *Chiquanous,* 31; and *Panurge,* 56; special faculty in *P.,* 59; learned man in *T.L.,* and loss of importance, 60; speculation on man's destiny, 60

Erasmus, 10; influence on R., 17; sneers at monks, 56

Francis I: effects of his despotic rule, 69; attitude towards students, 187

For EU product safety concerns, contact us at Calle de José Abascal, 56–1°,
28003 Madrid, Spain or eugpsr@cambridge.org.

www.ingramcontent.com/pod-product-compliance
Ingram Content Group UK Ltd.
Pitfield, Milton Keynes, MK11 3LW, UK
UKHW020806190625
459647UK00032B/1909